BOTTLE-CAP SUNDAES

BY

PATRICK M. SHERIDAN

ISBN: 1-4107-0419-X (e-book)
ISBN: 1-4107-0420-3 (Paperback)
ISBN: 1-4107-0421-1 (Dust jacket)

Library of Congress Control Number: 2002096604

This book is printed on acid free paper.

Printed in the United States of America
Bloomington, IN

1stBooks – rev. 1/21/03

This book is dedicated to my wife Diane
and to Mozart, Elvis, and Whoopi.

INTRODUCTION

There are thousands of Veterinarians and Other Experts who will tell you that dogs cannot talk. But in America, alone, there are 70 million Dog Owners who will disagree. Dog Owners have always talked to their pets and most of them know that their pets talk back.

And finally, three dogs have admitted to talking and are willing to go on record about it. In the following pages, Mozart, Whoopi, and Elvis share their views on the major events that shaped their lives.

Their candid and irreverent conversations provide insight into the humor, love, ambition, embarrassment, concern, and surprise— *emotions*—that all dogs experience.

PROLOGUE

We did not have a dog in our home in Detroit when I was growing up. In our family, if you wanted something to play with, you could always find a kid—if you wanted something to cuddle, you could always find a kid in diapers. I was the second oldest of twelve children.

When I was thirty, my first wife, Jane, and my daughter, Kelly, got a dog. They named it Woody. Woody was clearly their dog: they trained him, fed him, walked him, and played with him.

My only other experience with a dog came more than ten years later when we took in a lost dog—an old, red dachshund that had more gray hair than I did. The dog had been wandering our Baltimore neighborhood. We kept him in our home while we looked for his owner. Within a day or two, we found the owner and returned the dog.

I liked that old dachshund.

As best I can recall, that is my entire history from birth to age 51 with respect to dogs. By 51, I had remarried, and my wife Diane and I had moved to Indianapolis. Our children had also scattered from Baltimore and Boston to Chicago and Los Angeles. Diane and I were empty nesters. We decided to get a dog.

I had never been a "dog person." But that was about to change forever.

PART ONE

MOZART

PATRICK M. SHERIDAN

CHAPTER ONE

We found an ad in the Sunday paper and went to the home of a very nice couple that bred dachshunds. They had several puppies in a large box. As we looked in, one little guy started saying, "Take me, take me, take me...

"I'm the best, the softest, the friendliest. See how much my tail wags? That says how happy I am to see you. Wouldn't I be great to come home to after a hard day at work? How can you pass up a chance to adopt me?"

I said, "All the dogs look soft and friendly, and all the tails are wagging. You seem a little pushy. I think I'll check out the other dogs before I decide."

He continued to jump up and down. "*Okay*, I didn't want to have to play my trump card so early, but I can do tricks."

"What tricks do you perform?"

He grinned. "You have to listen more carefully. I didn't say that I actually *do* any tricks. I said I *can* do tricks, meaning I am *capable* of doing tricks once I've learned them." Then he muttered, half under his breath, "If that's what you want your dog to do...*Hell*, I'll sing 'The Sun Will Come Out Tomorrow' if it will get me out of here."

Well, I've always had a soft spot in my heart for irreverence. I lifted him out of the box. He loved this and licked my face. No one, especially a dog, had ever done this to me before, and I wasn't sure that I liked it. But his grinning made me laugh. I handed him to Diane and she instantly fell in love with him. So...we adopted him.

As we drove home, Diane and I discussed names. Our adoptee was sitting in her lap and joined in the conversation. "You are going to give me a classy name, right? Not one of those dog names. I won't answer to Spot or anything as common as that."

"Well, you don't have a spot, so we can rule that one out. What did *you* have in mind?" I asked.

"I'm just asking you to keep in mind that I'm a class act...not just some dog named Spot or Fido...You'll think of something appropriate."

Dachshunds have long bodies, long noses, long ears, and long tails, and very short legs. They can be long-haired or short-haired. Their hair color can be brown or black or red. Our new dog was short-haired and red—really a reddish brown—but what is called red.

Since he was a purebred dachshund, we decided to recognize his Austrian ancestry and named him Mozart after our favorite composer. Like the composer's music, he would fill our home with joy. And likewise, he would be a precocious little stinker.

He was so small that I could hold him in my hand—*and* he was like a kid in a candy store. On the day we brought him home, he never seemed to stop running. Whenever I set him down, he ran everywhere in the house, sniffed every inch, and got into everything he could reach.

We filled out the papers to register him, naming him Mozart Thunderhooves Sheridan. He became the first Canine-American member of our family.

That night, when I picked him up and sat with him on our king-size bed, he was thrilled. "This is great! This is the biggest bed I've ever seen." He jumped off my lap and ran laps around the mattress, then rolled on it. He was having the time of his life.

"Wow. This will be great! Just the three of us in this huge bed—*all this room*—I can't believe it. In my last house, they made all us dogs sleep in the same box."

"Now, don't get too excited Mozart, you are…"

He cut me off. "Is that a TV? This is too cool. Our own TV in the bedroom. Those other folks never let us watch TV…Dad…Mind if I call you Dad?…You've done great. This is even better than I had expected, and I was expecting a lot. You're the best!"

Mozart continued to run around the bed, jumping up on my lap, then back down again. When he saw the dog crate in the corner he stopped dead in his tracks.

"What's that?"

"That's where you sleep."

"What? You're putting me in the slammer? My first night here, and I'm in solitary confinement? Did they forget to give you an instruction manual? Even they never put us in the hole…I can't even see the TV from *there*."

"It's a nice crate and we put in a soft pad and a warm blanket for you to sleep on. You'll be safe and warm and comfortable."

When Mozart realized that the hard-line was not going to work, he tried to reason with me. "Dad, why don't we look at this logically? If you put me in that cage, you know I'm going to tear up the blanket and the pad. I'm not threatening to do it—*and I certainly don't want to do it*—but it's in my nature."

"I guess I better keep the blanket and pad out of the crate then."

"That's cold."

"Did I misunderstand you, Mozart?"

"No. I'm just saying that if you put any dog in a cage, he'll get bored and chew everything in sight. Put me on the bed and I'll be too happy to chew anything. What do you think?"

"I think you'll get used to it. Try it—you'll like it."

He looked like he was about to say, What are you, a comic? But he bit his tongue and tried one last approach. "Dad, we're a family. Wouldn't it be great if the whole family slept in the same bed? I could sleep between you guys near the foot of the bed, and you'd never even know I was there."

"I'd know."

"When you wanted to cuddle, I'd be there in a flash. Isn't that why you got me? And sleeping in the same bed will help us bond. Wouldn't hurt to do a little male bonding, right?"

"Wouldn't hurt to get a little sleep either, and now I'm going to sleep." I put him in his crate and got into bed. For the first few minutes, I could hear him muttering but couldn't hear what he said. Probably just as well...He slept like a rock till morning.

This arrangement lasted about a month. Mozart quietly worked on us...a hint here, a suggestion there. We'd bring him onto the bed when we were watching TV or reading, and we'd hold him or he'd lie next to one of us. Then he'd crawl toward the foot of the bed and say, "I'm just going to rest my eyes for a few minutes. I'm not really going to sleep on the bed, but if I ever did sleep on the bed, this would show you how quiet and inconspicuous I would be, if you would just let me sleep on the bed."

Finally, one night, we unexpectedly fell asleep with him there. When we woke, he was lying near the top of the bed, leaning his back against my shoulders and facing Diane. She said his eyes were closed, but that he had this big grin on his face. He knew he had won.

Mozart loves stuffed animals. Mostly, he loves ripping the stuffing out of them, but he plays with them long after that. His first stuffed animal was a white dog, larger than he was. We named it Butkus after the dog in *Rocky*. ...*Dick Butkus* may have been the greatest linebacker in NFL history, but *this* Butkus was no match for Mozart.

When I walked in the room, there was stuffing all over the floor. "Mozart, what a mess! What did you do?"

"Butkus and I were playing football. He was the Chicago Bears and I was the Dallas Cowboys. The Cowboys beat the stuffing out of the Bears, if you get my drift."

"I get your drift all right. How did you get to be the Cowboys? We live in Indianapolis."

"When Kevin was here last week, he told me that the Cowboys were the greatest team ever, so I'm the Cowboys. Butkus had no choice. He had to be the Bears."

"Good thinking."

"Kevin's from Chicago. I can't wait to show him what I did to Butkus, the famous Chicago Bear."

"I have to clean up this mess, and you've ruined Butkus."

"Actually, I've improved him. It was difficult pulling him around. He weighed much more than I did. Now, without the stuffing, he's a sleeker version, and it's much easier to carry him around."

"By the way, Kevin calls you Dad, and I call you Dad...So is Kevin like my brother or something?"

"Yeah, something like that. I am Kevin's dad. You're more like his stepbrother once removed. Although, in your case, the removed step is an entire species."

"So, what about Patrick, Jim, and Clyde? Are they my stepbrothers once removed?"

"Yes, they are."

"I like being a stepbrother once removed. That sounds impressive. I think I'll update my resume."

"You do that, Mozart."

Butkus became Mozart's constant companion. He constantly played with him, chewed on him, humped him, then fell asleep with him. In the long run, we were glad Mozart had taken the stuffing out since we threw Butkus into the washing machine dozens of times.

As soon as the vet said the timing was appropriate, we had Mozart neutered. While I fully supported the idea for all the health and humane reasons, I'm not the first guy who just didn't want to be personally involved if I didn't have to be. Diane was a nurse and better suited for this type of thing. She took him to the vet, but I knew that Mozart and I would eventually have to talk about it. We got into it that night.

"I'd like to see you alone," he whispered.

He was very subdued, and I picked him up. "Sure. Let's go into the study and I'll close the door."

"Do you know where Mom took me today while you were at work?"

"Yes."

"And what they did to me?"

"Yes."

"How could you let that happen?"

"It was for your own good. It was for the good of the whole family. We aren't going to be raising puppies. And it reduces your chance of testicular cancer and other diseases."

"Whatever happened to the old philosophy of 'if it ain't broke, don't fix it'? I wasn't broke was I?"

"No. You weren't. I can tell you, we won't ever do anything like that again...*and I am sorry*. How are you feeling? Did it hurt?"

"No. They knocked me out and I didn't feel a thing...Now, I'm sore and I'm still in shock."

"What were you thinking when you woke up?"

"The first thing I thought about was Garry Shandling. He does an entire routine on neutering a dog."

"I know. I've seen it."

"The dog says, 'Has anybody seen them? I had them when I left the house. I had them in the car, etc.' It's not nearly as funny as the audience seemed to think."

"I didn't realize you'd seen that."

7

"I was going to ask you about it, but by the time you got home that night, I forgot."

"When I was your age, I had my tonsils out. My mother gave me ice cream. Would some Haagen Dazs help?"

"Can't hurt. Might help. But if you're comparing losing your tonsils to what I lost today, you need to retake your sex education class, and this time, pay attention."

"They didn't have sex education when I went to school."

"Color me surprised."

"Let's take the ice cream to bed. I think your mother would like to hold you for a while."

If I had given a spoonful of ice cream to Mozart, he would have eaten it in a single gulp. So, I took the cap from a bottle of Coke and filled it with ice cream. It was the same amount of ice cream as a teaspoonful, but it took him a lot longer to lick it out of the bottle cap. We called it a bottle-cap sundae.

It had not been a happy day for any of us and we were eager to leave this day behind. Still, Diane and I were glad that Mozart had been neutered. And possibly, now that it has faded into a distant memory, I think even Mozart might agree that we did the right thing. On the other hand, I'm never going to ask him.

CHAPTER TWO

Diane and I occasionally traveled together. For the holidays we drove to Baltimore to visit our children and on vacations and business trips we patronized the airline industry.

As we approached our first airline flight since Mozart had joined our family, we faced a decision and resolved to leave Mozart at a nearby kennel owned by our vet. It was my task to tell him what was about to happen. He was sitting on my lap.

"Guess what, Moz…We're going to let you go to camp."

"What's camp?"

"Well, it's a place where all kinds of dogs get together for a few days, swap some stories, have some laughs, and have a great time. You'll love it."

"Will I know any of the other dogs?"

"You never know. Some of the dogs from the neighborhood might be there. At the very least, you'll make a lot of new friends."

"Is this like sending me away to military school?"

"Not at all. I think Patrick, Kevin, and Jim wanted to go to camp when they were young, but I wasn't able to send them."

"So, you didn't send your own sons to camp, but you're sending me?"

"What can I say? I've told you that you are special."

"Do I get my own king-size bed?"

"I doubt it, but I believe you'll have your very own semi-private room."

"Do you have a camp brochure or anything?"

"This camp doesn't print a brochure. Here's the kicker—they try to keep this quiet—but there will be female dogs there."

He perked up some and gave me a slight grin.

"Well, since you have gone to all this trouble and have made all the arrangements for me to go to camp, I'll give it a try. Can I take Butkus?"

"Sure, why not?"

"When am I going?"

"Tomorrow morning."

"I never had a choice, did I?"

9

"Not on this one."

"Okay. Anything good on TV tonight?"

"Yeah, CBS is running some new dog food commercials."

The next morning, Diane buckled Mozart's collar around his neck, packed up his blanket, and headed for the car. Mozart carried Butkus in his mouth and left for his first day at dog camp.

We got home on a Sunday night. On my way to work the next morning, I accompanied Diane to pick up Mozart. I have never seen him so happy to see us. Everything south of his ears was frantically wagging back and forth. We were just as glad to see him.

"Why, Mozart, is that a tear in your eye?" I asked.

"Don't even go there."

"Okay, I'll see you tonight, and you can tell me all about camp." I could hardly wait to hear the war stories.

When I arrived home that evening, he was happy to see me and was wagging his tail, but he had a strange look on his face.

"Well, Mozart, tell me all about camp."

"Camp? You call that camp? The other dogs called it a kennel. It comes from an old German word which means solitary confinement with noise."

"None of the other dogs have any imagination. I thought you'd make more out of the opportunity."

"Pat and Kevin and Jim never wanted to go to camp, did they? They're too smart for that. Where was camp for them anyway? Attica?"

"Didn't you see any pretty female dogs that you could make friends with?"

"Oh, sure, there was one just down the row from me. All I had to do to make eye contact with her was to stand on my hind legs so I could see over the Doberman and the German shepherd between us."

"How was the food?"

"Give me a break. It was awful. All they had was that scientifically correct stuff. You know the stuff I mean. The stuff that Mom sets out every day, hoping I'll eventually try it. If they had ice cream, they never gave me any. They never even let me lick the bowl."

"You must have enjoyed making friends and swapping stories with the other dogs. That was fun, wasn't it?"

"First of all, no one believed a word I said. When I mentioned that my cage door, at home, is always open and that I only go into the cage when I want to—and that I use it primarily to keep my toys in—they all started giggling."

"I hadn't thought of that."

"When I told them we ate cookies and ice cream while we watched TV, they *howled* in laughter."

"They didn't believe that either?"

"No, and when I said I slept in the king-size bed with you guys, they held their stomachs and begged me to stop."

"What kind of stories did they tell?"

"None. Every time one of them started to tell a story, the rest would shout him down with 'Let's hear another one from Mozart!'"

"Did you tell them any more?"

"I wasn't going to, but then they asked me where Butkus slept. When I said, 'in the bed with us,' they were rolling on the floor and said I should get an agent."

"So, you were a big hit. You'll probably show up in the yearbook as funniest guy in the class. I bet they are all looking forward to seeing you again next time."

His face turned white. "Next time? *Next time?* Dad, we need to talk. Seriously. You thought I'd have a semi-private room?...*Only my thoughts* were private."

"It couldn't have been that bad."

"It was. I was in the hole the entire time. We only got a few minutes a day in the yard. They say trustees get extra yard time, but no one seems to know how to make trustee. This was hard time."

"I'm sorry you had a bad experience."

"You know how I usually hide under the bed if I even think I might get a bath?... I *asked* Mom for a bath today."

"You're kidding."

"Take my word for it, had you sent Patrick to camp, you wouldn't even be on his Christmas card list."

"Was there anything at all that you liked?"

"This morning, when they brought me into the lobby and I saw you and Mom... That was the single best moment of my life. I was totally *verklempt.*"

"You've got to stop watching so much 'Saturday Night Live.'"

11

"Well, I was very happy you sprung me."

"In the future, we'll see if there is some other alternative when we have to travel and can't take you with us."

"By the way, where did you guys go?"

"We went to Orlando."

"Orlando? You went to Disney World? That's like Dog Heaven. Don't you watch 'The World of Disney' on Sunday night? That's the home of Goofy, and Pluto, and 101 Dalmatians, and Lady and the Tramp, and the Fox and the Hound. Why didn't you take me with you?"

"It just wouldn't have worked out. Sorry about that, Mozart."

"I'll tell you one thing I learned from spending a weekend at your camp."

"What's that?"

"There's no place like home."

"That was a lesson worth learning. Some folks spend a whole lifetime without really appreciating that fact."

When we went to bed that night, Mozart crawled up to the top of the bed and flopped on my pillow. "God, it's good to be home," he said.

That night Mozart and I both went to sleep grinning.

Mozart was born on Halloween. As his first birthday approached, Diane wanted to get him something special. She may have overdone it. Diane bought him a sweater for his birthday and a costume hat to wear on Halloween. Mozart hated them both from the minute she put them on him. He came running in to see me.

"Have you seen what Mom got me for my birthday?"

"Yes, you look cute. Happy birthday."

"I look ridiculous. If you take me out for a walk on Halloween while I'm wearing this outfit I'll run away. The other dogs in the neighborhood will needle me unmercifully."

"Lighten up. It's only a sweater. It'll keep you warm. It's getting cold outside."

"I'm a dog. We come with our own sweater. *This one* is butt ugly. Look at it."

"I'll admit that's a lot of colors for a sweater…It looks like it fits well. How does it feel?"

"How do you think it feels? It has straps that go under the tail. It feels like a thong. How many of your sweaters tie under the crotch?"

He had me there. Actually, I was already on his side. "Okay," I said, "here's the deal. Everybody gets stuff on their birthdays that they would never buy for themselves. Usually, it's clothes. Closets everywhere are full of ties and sweaters that have never been worn. So just go along with it. Wear it when we leave, and I'll remove it before we get out of the driveway."

On Halloween, Mozart actually flicked off the hat as he walked through the door. We never put it on him again. I never had to remove the sweater either. It covered his torso for the first few steps and his hindquarters for the next few. Finally, he stepped on it and it slid off completely.

When we got back from our walk, we split a whole cup of Haagen Dazs vanilla ice cream for his birthday and broke out the real birthday presents: the dog toys. Mozart got toys that he could chew, squeak, or throw through the air and chase. He had a great birthday.

"Thanks a million. This has been the kind of birthday I've always dreamed of, except, of course, no one could have ever dreamed up that hat and sweater."

"You're welcome. Now get to sleep…We'll play with your toys again tomorrow."

"Maybe next year I'll have my birthday in July. Then no one will think to buy me a Halloween costume—and no one wears sweaters in the summer."

"Your birthday will always be on Halloween, but we won't put costumes on you anymore…You might appreciate the sweater a little more when it gets cold in the winter."

"Not bloody likely," he muttered, then fell asleep.

CHAPTER THREE

As Mozart grew older, he began to look less like a puppy and more like a dog. His body began to lengthen until finally he had the traditional look of his breed—that stretched out look that has earned dachshunds the nickname "wiener dogs." Mozart also began to behave more like a dog—meaning I was about to find out a few things the hard way.

One day when Mozart and I were home alone, he chewed a hole in the living room carpet. Since I had no previous experience with dogs—Mozart being my first and only—this situation would mark my first confrontation with any dog, *ever*. It also would mark the last serious confrontation that Mozart and I would ever have.

I saw the hole as soon as I entered the living room. *"Mozart!"* I yelled. Whereupon, Mozart ran underneath the couch. I yelled again. *"Mozart, come out from under there!"* Wisely, he knew that this was not the best move he might make.

But ignorance prevailed—*my own*. I got down on my hands and knees and reached under the couch to pull him out. As my hand closed in on him, he bit. He didn't bite and hold, but he bit hard, leaving a mark right behind my thumb. Suddenly I realized that, while I didn't know the right thing to do, attempting to pull him out was probably the dumbest. I stood and left the room.

Eventually, Mozart slowly walked into the study and over to the chair where I sat. "Is your hand all right?" he asked.

"Yeah, it's sore but I'll live."

"Do you want to talk about it?"

"I suppose we better. Come here..." I picked him up, carefully, and sat him on my lap.

He looked up into my face. "I'm sorry I bit you, but that's what I do when I'm cornered and threatened."

"Yeah, I figured that out. I've never even seen a dog bite anyone before...hadn't even occurred to me that..."

"Live and learn."

"Very funny...Actually that *is* very funny."

"Why did you *yell* at me?" Mozart asked.

"Because you chewed up the carpeting."

"Why were you reaching for me?"

"I wanted to pull you out from under the couch."

"What were you going to do when you got me out?"

"I don't know, but I didn't feel like talking to you while you were under there."

"You seemed pretty ticked off."

"Well, I was. Why did you chew up the carpeting? You have a crate full of dog toys, most of them chewable."

"You can never have too many interesting things to chew. It was kind of fun, unraveling the carpet a thread at a time...You probably don't want to hear all this, do you?"

"No, I don't. And I don't want you to ever chew the rug again, got it?"

"I got it...probably. All right, I'll try to remember never to do it again."

"I'm sorry I yelled at you. I was pretty ticked off. That won't happen again."

"I'm sorry I bit you. I was pretty scared. That won't happen again either."

Mozart then turned so that my left arm supported him and his head lay against my chest. This was his favorite position. My right hand caressed his ear and neck. In about 30 seconds his breathing grew heavy and he fell asleep.

In the nine years since that day, Mozart has never bitten me again, nor has he bitten anyone else for that matter. Neither have I yelled at him again in anger. Furthermore, he has only chewed two more holes in the carpeting, and fortunately, the carpet repair folks have fixed them so that we don't even notice.

In Indianapolis, we lived in a small, one-level house. Mozart could run a lap that started in the bedroom, continued through the study, hooked left through the living room, and stretched out through the kitchen/dining room to the far end of the living room and down a short hallway back to the bedroom where he had started. This nonstop route took him through the entire house, except for a couple of spare rooms used only when our kids stayed overnight.

Our house faced a 135-acre, manmade lake, which was previously a rock quarry. Mozart liked to sit on the floor and stare at the lake through the sliding-glass doors that opened onto our deck. From the deck, a short set of steps led down to the pier where we kept our pontoon.

I was gone every day from 6:30 a.m. until 7:00 p.m., and during those hours, Mozart and Diane were inseparable. They did everything together—ran errands, watched TV, took naps. But when I got home, Mozart and I would play until he was exhausted.

Diane had dubbed me the "funmeister."

Every night, Mozart and I walked down to the pier to feed the ducks. There were about a dozen of them that appeared every night. I took pieces of bread, broke them up, and tossed them while Mozart barked. We did this most evenings from spring when the ducks first arrived until fall when they left for the winter.

In addition to the ducks, there were also a few catfish that came up to the pier. They wanted what the ducks missed. But since the ducks were pretty good at recovering any pieces that sunk into the water, the catfish rarely got anything.

"You having fun, Mozart?"

"Yeah, this is the greatest. I love folks my own size."

"What's with all the barking?"

"I'm trying to find a common language. I don't quack and they don't seem to speak English."

"Why are you so loud?"

"They don't seem to understand me, so I thought I'd ratchet up the volume."

"Is that working?"

"Not yet. I got the idea from Jim. He said that when you went to France, you tried speaking French and that when none of the locals understood a word you said, you tried talking louder."

"It didn't work there either. What are you trying to say?"

"I'm trying to convince some of them to come up onto the pier so they will be closer to you and will get more of the bread, hee, hee, hee."

"Mozart, chortling does not become you. Anyway, it appears they are not falling for your line of bull."

"It was worth a shot. Hey, what's with the catfish? They slink around and hardly ever get any bread."

"They eat whatever falls to the bottom. They are bottom feeders. Maybe they've always been like that. I don't know much about catfish."

"You don't suppose they'd like to come up onto the pier to get closer to the bread, do you?"

"They can't get up without my help and I'm not going to catch them just for your amusement. Anyway, I just ran out of bread."

"I'd rather catch a duck anyway. If I can't talk them into coming up here by next week, I'll work on a plan to trick them instead."

"I'm sure you will. Here, let me carry you up the stairs. Diane keeps reminding me that stairs are not good for your long back and short legs."

"I always appreciate the lift, but I can do without the short jokes."

The next time Diane and I planned a trip, we decided to try a dogsitting service. For about the cost of a day in the kennel, a person would come to our home twice a day to feed Mozart, let him out, and play with him. I told Mozart about our plans.

"Mozart, we are going away for the weekend."

"Oh man! *You can't be thinking*—don't even go there—the idea of it is too traumatic. I really don't want to go to the kennel. I don't even want to hear the word *camp* again."

"Well, we are willing to try something different if we can agree on a few ground rules."

"Like what?"

"You can stay here in the house while we are gone. You can sleep in your crate at night, like you do now during the day. You can watch the ducks through the sliding-glass doors and you'll have all your toys to play with."

"How will I eat?"

"A sitter will come by twice a day. He'll feed you and let you play in the yard, but we are closing the gate so you can't go down to the pier."

"This is a great idea, Dad. Where do I sign?…Wait. There's *a catch* somewhere, isn't there?"

"Only a few rules. If you eat the carpeting or the furniture or anything else in the house, other than your dog toys, you will go have to go to the kennel next time. And next time, we will not pay for first-class accommodations."

"I had first-class? I'd hate to think what the low-rent district looked like."

"How many cages do you think they have?" I asked. "When they run out of cages, I think they put all the remaining dogs in one big cell."

"You're making this up, aren't you?"

"I think they just dump the food in there also. It's sort of first come, first serve and the big dogs get all the good stuff."

"You mean I'd become a bottom feeder, like the catfish in the lake."

"Excellent analogy. It shouldn't happen though, not if you behave yourself while we're gone."

"No worries, mates. Everything will be shipshape when you get back."

"I see...*Crocodile Dundee* must have been on TV again today. Well, I'm not kidding. Whether or not we do it this way again will depend on what we find when we get home on Sunday."

The next day, as we packed for our trip, Mozart kept walking around, singing "Master of the House, Keeper of the Zoo" from *Les Miserables*. Being left alone and in charge of the house was pretty heady stuff for young Mozart.

Sunday night, when he heard our car pulling into the driveway, he came running to the door. As we entered the house his tail wagged furiously and he ran around in circles. I put down my bags and picked him up. We walked through the house, which to my surprise, was in excellent shape. It looked as if we had only been gone a few hours. The sitter had left a note indicating that all had gone well.

"What do you think? Looks pretty good, right?"

"Well, Mozart, this seems to have worked out very well. I'm very proud of you."

"You know what they say...If you want to run with the big dogs, etc., etc."

"You're not that big of a dog."

"Big enough to be left in charge and not let you down."

"That is true, Mozart. That is true. I presume you preferred the dogsitter to the kennel."

"Absolutely. Except for being lonesome, this was much better than the kennel. I missed you guys and missed sleeping in our bed, but I loved being home."

"Any other problems besides being lonesome?"

"Just one. Some of the ducks noticed that we weren't coming down to the pier. When I looked out the window at them, they started making fun of me. They were laughing and having a great time. Someday, they'll find out that paybacks are hell."

"So, if you could have gone outside and if you hadn't been lonesome, then everything would have been almost perfect?"

"That's about it."

"Well, Mom and I have a couple of ideas that you might find interesting. But we'll save those for another day...In any event, you should be very proud of yourself. I certainly am. In fact, I think this calls for a bottle-cap sundae. Let's get the Haagen Dazs and go to bed."

That night, with Mozart flopped up against me as usual, I thought of how proud I really was of him. Throughout the night, he occasionally wagged his tail. He was definitely as glad as we were to be back in our own bed.

PATRICK M. SHERIDAN

PART TWO

THE TWINS

PATRICK M. SHERIDAN

CHAPTER FOUR

When Mozart was about two years old, we decided that it would be good for him to have some canine company and we started looking for another dog.

My oldest daughter, Mary, and I often think alike and act alike, and we have the same irreverent sense of humor. She is as close to a clone of me as you can find. She was, therefore, still getting used to the idea that, in my fifties, I had even one dog, and she could not believe it when she heard I might get a second. She and I had lived under the same roof for more than 20 of my non-dog years. Incredulous, she called me. "Patrick says you are looking for a new dog. What happened to Mozart?"

"Nothing. He gets lonesome when he is alone, so we are going to get him a playmate."

"Let me see if I got this straight. You're actually going to get a dog for your dog?"

"Yes, we are."

"Unbelievable."

From that day on, when she introduced me as her father, she would add, "But this is *not* the man who raised me."

Diane found another ad in the Sunday paper, and we drove to a farmhouse about an hour south of Indianapolis. Since Mozart was a male, we had decided that the new dog should be a female. There were only two dogs left—one female and one male, black, miniature dachshund. Mozart was a red, standard and had grown to full size, about 25 pounds. These dogs would grow to about 15 pounds each.

They were the smallest puppies I had ever seen and except for their sex, you could not tell them apart. They were adorable. The two ran around and wrestled with each other. When they stopped playing, I picked up the female. She had the cutest face. She looked right into my eyes and asked, "Can we go home with you?"

"Well, you can and you will," I said.

"Me too, me too, me too!" came a voice from the crate.

The female continued to look directly into my eyes—not in a challenging way—but to make sure we stayed connected. Mozart

23

almost never did this. He would stare at me *only until* I turned my face toward him; then he would turn to his toys, to the door, or to whatever he wanted to show me. Most of the time, when I held Mozart, he would be looking around—unless he wanted to make sure I was listening to him. Then he would look me directly in the eyes.

The female was so pretty. She didn't even blink as she said, "Can my brother come too?"

"Yeah, me too, me too, me too," came the voice from the crate.

"Well, we were looking for a female, since we already have a male dog."

"Not like my brother," she said. "He really has a big heart. He'll be a great dog for you. Besides, he needs me. I kind of look after him. I'd really appreciate it if he could come with us."

Diane picked up the male. He was awfully cute too. He was grinning, and his tail was wagging a mile a minute. "Can I come too? Can I come too?" he kept asking.

"OK," said Diane.

"We'll take them both," we told the farmers. The puppies started to lick our faces. Diane didn't like that, so she held the male puppy down against her chest so he couldn't reach her face. The female was rubbing the top of her head against my chin, licking me, and making me laugh. I didn't care about the licking.

When she stopped, again she looked straight into my eyes. "Thank you. You won't regret this. We are going to have a great time together."

"You're welcome. Now let's get your stuff and go home. We have a surprise waiting for you."

I have been an admirer of Whoopi Goldberg for as long as I can remember. I was a fan when she was first doing stand-up comedy, long before she began making movies and television appearances. She always makes me laugh. In her honor, Diane and I named our beautiful, little, black, female puppy, Whoopi.

We named the male Elvis. While most people think of Elvis Presley as the King, I've always thought of him as the ultimate Good Ole Boy. He loved his mama and his heritage and his country and his friends. He was a poor boy, come to greatness, and he remained, to the end, a good ole boy at heart. We didn't know it at the time, but our Elvis would turn out to be the greatest Good Ole Boy Canine-American that ever lived.

When we got home with the twins, we let them run into the house. Mozart had been sleeping in the study by the window, so he hadn't heard us drive up. Suddenly, the twins were all over him—licking him, pawing him, and jumping at him. They loved him immediately. The feeling was not mutual. He came running toward the garage.

"Dad, come quick. We have dogs in here. Help me round them up, so we can get rid of them."

"We don't want to get rid of them."

"*Very funny.* Seriously, we have to move quickly, before they get into everything. They could break things or chew things—*or worse.*"

"I'm not worried. All *my* things are up, out of the way."

"Oh, great. Here we are in the midst of a crisis and you're going to start with the short jokes. Get a grip. These are just puppies. I bet they aren't even house trained."

"You weren't house trained, but we survived."

By now the twins had checked out all the rooms in the house. They found us in the living room.

"Hey, there you are," said Whoopi. "This place is *enormous.* What a *cool* house."

"Yes, I guess it is. By the way, let me do the introductions. This is Mozart. He's in a state of shock right now, but when he comes out of it, he'll be the best friend you guys could ever have. Mozart, this is Whoopi and her brother Elvis."

"Hi Mozart," they said, nearly in unison.

Whoopi and Elvis jumped at Mozart and tried to climb on top of him. He wasn't having any of it and ran into the bedroom. They chased after him. Ditching them for a minute, Mozart rejoined me in the living room.

"Seriously, Dad, we have to get rid of these dogs."

"Mozart, they are now a part of our family. You'll learn to love them."

"But they are following me everywhere. They jump on me and lick me and won't leave me alone."

"Now, Mozart, let me see if I can think of a similar experience..."

"Come on, there's no comparison. You love it when I do those things to you."

Before he could say another word, Whoopi came running and Mozart raced to the bedroom with her hot on his heels. Elvis walked over and looked up at me.

"What a beautiful house. Do you really live here? Is this really your home?"

I sat down on the floor and picked him up. "No, Elvis, this is really *our* home. And you, and Whoopi, are also going to live here for as long as Mom, Mozart, and I do."

"Honest to God?" he whispered.

"Honest to God, Elvis. Welcome home."

Tears came to his eyes. Then he put his head on my chest and fell asleep.

CHAPTER FIVE

If you have learned to house train one dog, you have only learned to house train one dog. There is no magical "one strategy fits all." When we trained Mozart, it was relatively simple. We cut a deal.

"Mozart, we are going to house train you."

"You're going to house train me? Why not train me to do a few tricks, so I can be on TV?"

"You are going to learn to go outside to pee. There will be a newspaper on the floor in the spare bathroom if we are gone for a long time, or in case of an emergency."

"I understand. So what's in it for me?"

"You'll continue to live with us. We'll continue to feed you. You might not be returned to sleeping in the crate."

"Whoa, Dad. I'm sensing some negative vibes here. Sounds like somebody had a bad day at work and forgot that we leave those feelings at work."

"Maybe you're right."

"Look, all I'm saying is that I presume this means less work for you, so how about a little something extra for the kid. After all, I'm the one who is going into training."

"What do you have in mind?"

"Now you're talking. How about three, squeaky stuffed animals and a pint of Haagen-Dazs?"

"How about one, squeaky stuffed animal and a bottle-cap sundae? If you go a week without an accident, I'll give you another."

"Okay. It's a deal."

Mozart was trained without a great deal of effort and fairly quickly. Actually, this is easy for me to say since Diane did the training.

Since his house training, I don't believe Mozart has ever had an "accident." I feel confident in saying this because, on those many occasions when he has relieved himself in a place where we do not want him to, it has been no accident. When I am away on an overnight business trip, his favorite spot is to pee on the throw rug that I stand on when shaving. This is *no* accident.

"Mozart, you peed on my rug while I was out of town."

"Me? Don't you mean Elvis? You know he'll pee anywhere."

"This wasn't Elvis. It has your DNA."

"Let me think. You know, I might have been thinking about how much I missed you last night when I had no one to play with and *thought* I was standing on the paper."

"Not likely. The paper is in the other bathroom. Don't do it again."

"OK. You know, I wasn't even aware that dog pee had DNA."

"Neither was I."

"I can't believe I fell for that one."

House training Whoopi was a piece of cake. She understood what we wanted and did it almost immediately. She was delighted just to get hugs and recognition for her accomplishments. Her heart was always in the right place. Unlike Mozart, she's never had an accident, intentional or otherwise.

Elvis, on the other hand, turned out to be a significant challenge. He wasn't rebellious or recalcitrant. He just never seemed to get the concept.

"Elvis, come on. We're going outside to pee."

"You mean you're going to start peeing outside?"

"Well, no. I'm not, but you are."

"I want to be like you, Dad. You're my hero. I'll pee in the house."

"Actually, no you won't. You are going to learn to pee outside like Mozart and Whoopi do."

"Okay. Whatever you say."

"Well, come on. We're going outside."

"But, I don't have to go now."

"Elvis, come *now*."

I held the door open for him as he walked across the kitchen toward me. He peed on the floor the entire trip.

"Elvis, what are you doing? I thought you didn't have to go."

"Well, all this talk about peeing got me thinking about it. I guess I had to go after all."

According to Mozart, it was worse when we weren't home. Mozart found Elvis peeing in the front hall. This is the conversation as it was reported:

"What are you doing?" asked Mozart.

"I have to pee," said Elvis.

"We're supposed to wait until Mom and Dad get home and then go outside."

"I have to pee now."

"Then we're supposed to go on the newspaper in the spare bathroom."

"I'm *here*. The bathroom is way down the hall. No one will ever notice anyway."

"No one will notice? Elvis, they walk right through here when they come in."

"It'll be dry by then."

"You're going to get in trouble," warned Mozart.

"I won't get in trouble. I'll be in the bedroom. I'm no dummy. I'm not going to wait around here. When they come home, you and Whoopi will be here, wagging your tails like you always do. No one will ever know I did it."

"Elvis, there are only three of us here. I think Whoopi could wait a week to pee if she had to. And I never pee here. If I'm mad, I pee on Dad's rug."

"Look, Mozart, if the floor is still wet here and I'm in the bedroom, no one will ever figure out that I'm the one who did it. I know that *I'd* never figure it out."

"Elvis, there aren't enough books to list all the things that you can't figure out."

When we got home, I picked Elvis up in the bedroom and carried him to the front hall. "Did you do this?" I asked.

"Did you notice that I was in the bedroom?"

"I know you were in the bedroom. Did you do this before you went to the bedroom?"

"Wow. That's an excellent question. By the way, where were Mozart and Whoopi when you came home?"

"Never mind that."

"How was the movie, Dad? Did you give it a big 'thumbs up'? It's great to see you, Dad. I missed you. Boy, I'm glad you made it home safe."

"Elvis, did you do this?"

"Let me think. I've been in the bedroom for a long time. I might have done it before that. I can't be positive."

"Yeah, right, OK. Don't do it again. Now, let's go outside and pee before we go to bed."

"That's OK, Dad. I don't have to go anymore."

CHAPTER SIX

Shortly after the twins were house trained, they approached me about their sleeping arrangements. I was sitting on the couch when Whoopi jumped up, walked over, sat down on my lap, and looked up at me. "Hi Dad, do you have a minute to talk?" Elvis stood against my leg until I picked him up and set him next to us.

"Yes, I do. What's up?"

"Well, Elvis and I could not help but notice that Mozart sleeps in the bed with you and Mom, while we sleep in the cage on the floor…We couldn't help but notice because every morning he looks down from the bed and tells us how comfortable it was for him all night in the bed. Then he asks us how things are behind bars."

The fact is that Mozart loves the twins, although he does not often show it. He needles them a lot, as he does when he wakes up in the morning. On a good day, he'll admit that they are a lot of fun, but then he'll say, "Don't ever tell them I said that or it will go to their heads." Yet, whenever he is going to do something fun, he makes sure they know about it so that they can join him.

And, of course, Whoopi and Elvis just adore Mozart. They follow him everywhere. He is their hero. They look up to him—not only as a big brother—but also as a friend, a teacher, and a protector.

"Anyway," continued Whoopi, "we think perhaps it's time we sleep in the bed with you. It's such a large bed. When we've been there with you and Mom, it's seemed like there was plenty of room for all of us."

"Well, I suppose it will be all right. I'll clear it with Mom when she gets home. But you better *let me break it to Mozart*. I'll do that after clearing it with Mom."

Whoopi was delighted. She curled up with her head tucked under my chin.

Elvis went looking for Mozart.

"Hey, Mozart, I know something you don't know."

"Elvis, if I had complete amnesia, you still wouldn't know anything that I don't know."

31

"I know a secret."

"Your secrets consist of where you hid some toy, which I will find the first time I walk around the house, because it's usually in a doorway."

"Not this time. Only me, Whoopi, and Dad know this secret."

"You told Dad your secret? Did he laugh?"

"No, *he told me the secret.* And I'm not saying another word because he said I can't talk to you about it yet."

By now, Mozart was curious and came looking for me. In the meantime, Diane had come home and I had discussed the arrangement with her. She thought it was a good idea. Diane was easy.

Mozart was shocked. "*What* are you saying? We are going to let the dogs sleep in the bed with us? I spend my whole life working my way to the top of the food chain, and now I have to sleep with barnyard animals."

"Mozart, your whole life is less than three years, and Whoopi and Elvis are not barnyard animals." He cut me off.

"Three dog years is a very long time in human years. In fact, I'd be way past puberty by now if you hadn't had all my equipment removed."

"Don't start with that Mozart. Any guilt I used to feel stopped when neither Whoopi nor Elvis whined nearly as much as you did."

"Oh, sure, Little Miss Perfect with her 'Whatever you think is best, Dad' malarkey. And Elvis was probably relieved that he didn't have to figure out what to do or how to make things work."

"Anyway, they are going to sleep in the bed with us."

"How did they get sprung anyway? Isn't there supposed to be some kind of a probation hearing? I should have been allowed to speak out on behalf of the state against their release."

"Moz, in this house, I *am* the state. Your objections are heard, understood, appreciated, and now, will be completely ignored."

"OK, but if either of them lays one paw on my body during the night…just never mind."

That night, they all went to bed early, when Diane did, which was a couple of hours before me. It actually worked out very well. We each staked out our territory, or in the case of Whoopi, her multiple territories.

Mozart was in the habit of sleeping on the right side of the bed with me, but until I arrived, he would sleep in the middle of the bed. Then, once I got settled, he would walk over, line up next to my back and sort of parallel park—only it was more like parallel parachuting. He flopped against me, letting gravity take its course until he was nestled comfortably against me on the bed.

"Mozart, remind me to drop a 25-pound bag of sand on *your* back someday. I want you to experience the fun I have every night when you lay down with me."

"I'm trying to toughen you up, make a man out of you, hee-hee-hee."

"Very funny. Are you quite comfortable now?"

"I think I can get a little closer," he said, pushing harder against me.

"All right, knock it off and get some sleep."

Whoopi is a lighter sleeper than Mozart. Until I come to bed, she sleeps on my pillow. But as soon as I open the bedroom door, her tail starts thumping.

"I have your pillow nice and soft for you."

"Thanks for softening it up for me, Whoopi."

As soon as I am settled in, she curls against my face. She never does this exactly the same way any two nights in a row. Sometimes, she lies against my face. More often she lies on top of it. And much to my amazement, sometimes, she twists and turns until I feel my cheek on top of her head.

"Are you settled yet?"

"Almost…there…yes…now I am. Goodnight Dad."

"Goodnight Whoopi."

Her sleep ritual is fascinating. As soon as I fall asleep, or as soon as she thinks I have fallen asleep, she gets up and heads over to Diane and cuddles with her. She wakes up next to Diane every morning.

And Elvis? I think Elvis could sleep through Desert Storm. He loves to sleep. I think he even liked to sleep in the crate, but when Whoopi made her case for sleeping on the bed, he decided to "go with the flow." Elvis sleeps at the foot of the bed, exactly in the middle, as far away from the rest of us as possible, while still remaining on the mattress. He has no interest in flopping, curling, or cuddling with

33

anybody. He just likes to sleep and wants to minimize the likelihood that someone might disturb him.

"Goodnight Elvis. Are you okay down there?"

"ZZZZZZZZZZ"

CHAPTER SEVEN

When it comes to food, Elvis doesn't need to be catered to. He has never missed a meal. If he so much as hears Diane open the refrigerator door, he runs to the kitchen and sits next to her feet.

"I'm sitting right here, Mom, if you're looking for me."

"I see you Elvis."

"Well, you know how you sometimes have Dad's dinner ready, but then you can't find him? You don't have to worry about that with me. I won't keep you waiting."

"Just a minute, Elvis. It's almost ready."

"You're a great cook, Mom. Nobody makes baloney or chicken as good as you."

When Elvis finishes his food, he always checks out the other bowls to see if Whoopi or Mozart has left anything. Whoopi never cares much about eating. She rarely gets hungry, waits until Diane calls to tell her that snick-snacks are ready, and rarely finishes her food.

There are other differences as well. Elvis is less affectionate than Whoopi or Mozart. He is quite content to sit on the corner of the couch or lay at the foot of the mattress—just so long as he is included. Walking down to the dock or getting into the car to go to the park make him happiest. Yet, when we pick him up and hold him, he moans and looks like he has just found heaven on earth.

Whoopi is the least shy about asking for affection. If Diane or I are sitting, she will run and jump on a lap, then curl up, just as if she belongs there. When I come through the door, she wants to be picked up and held, unlike Mozart, who wants to play, and Elvis who wants to find out what we're going to do or when we're going to eat again.

So I pick up Whoopi and ask, "What did you do today?"

"Watched Oprah with Mom."

"How was Oprah?"

"Great. Doctor Phil was her guest. Mom and I think he is her best guest. He is really smart."

"Smarter than me?"

"I think you're smarter," she says, starting to lick my chin. "But Mom says Doctor Phil is smarter."

Even though Elvis is a miniature dachshund, he quickly grew to about twenty-five pounds—about Mozart's size. Whoopi is half as big and a ball of energy. She could jump higher, run faster, play longer than the others, and she never seemed to need rest.

Five mornings a week, I left for work early, before the others got up. Mozart and Elvis never knew I was leaving, but Whoopi and Diane were always awake to say goodbye.

While I was up early during the week, on weekends, I always slept in. This was never a problem with Mozart, as he was happy to sleep for as long as I did. Elvis was even more accommodating, since no matter how late I slept, he wanted to sleep longer. Whoopi, however, would have gloried at boot camp. From the minute she awoke, she was raring to go. Tail thumping furiously, she ran across the bed, put her front paws on my chest and stared at me before starting to lick my face. Weekends had become very different since Whoopi started sleeping on the bed.

"Hey, Dad, wake up. The sun is up. Rise and shine."

"Are you nuts, Whoopi? Go back to sleep."

"Come on. We slept all night. Look at me!" Lick...lick...thump...thump...

"Whoopi, go away. Everybody else is asleep. Be quiet."

"I know. This can be our private time." Lick...lick...thump...thump... "By the way, you need a shave."

I looked into her eyes. She was so intense. She continued to lick my face and thump her tail. I began to laugh.

"What's so funny? I'm serious. Let's go...Up and at 'em. What do you need, a cliché to get you going? If it will help, pick one. The early bird gets...A rolling stone gathers...Early to bed, early to rise makes a man healthy, wealthy, and wise..."

"Why are you standing on my chest? I thought cats did that."

"It's a good attention getter. Cats don't have exclusive rights to it. They just deserve credit for perfecting it."

By now, we have awakened Diane. She asks what we are doing and why I am laughing.

"Nothing. Sorry. Our little ball of energy just wants to get an early start, but it's not happening today...Whoopi, lie down next to me for a while. I'm going back to sleep. If you are real quiet and let me sleep, I'll take you to the park this afternoon."

Her tail starts thumping against the bed again. She murmurs, "Mission accomplished," as she falls back to sleep.

Two hours later, we are all awake.

"Dad says we are going to the park today," announces Whoopi with glee.

"Does he really? Hurray! Let's go!" shout Mozart and Elvis, who hit the floor running.

"In a while. We'll wait a little while until all the soccer and baseball games are over and the crowd is gone."

Our house on the lake had a very small lot. The sunroom off the master bedroom came right to the edge of the lake, and when you walked out the sliding glass door from the family room and onto the deck, you could drop bread over the railing to the fish and the ducks, which I did every time I saw fishermen coming. Our courtyard included the deck on the lakeside and about ten feet of space between our house and the property line of our neighbor's yard.

Because our deck and courtyard were so small, we all loved the park. Weather permitting, we went to the park—at least once—every weekend. There were a lot of games on Saturday morning, but hardly anyone was there after that. And the baseball diamonds were terrific because they were fenced in and once I had closed the gates, I could take off the leashes. It was the only time the dogs ran free. Often, they split up. But since it was all open space, I could play with any one of them and still watch after the others every few seconds.

Rarely did we see other dogs or people. When *they* did, they got very excited. Their tails wagged and they barked incessantly. Most dogs ignored them. Most people asked where I got a leash with three branches.

Once, when we went inside a baseball diamond, I shut, but, inadvertently, did not lock the gate; so it could be pushed open from the outside. A very large black dog came in. He towered over Whoopi and was at least twice the size of Elvis or Mozart. Before I had even noticed him, he was standing over Whoopi, who lay silently cowering on the ground about twenty yards from where Elvis and I were playing.

Elvis and I saw the dog at the same time. But before I could take a single step, Elvis had covered half the distance. He was running faster than I had ever seen him run. About three feet from the dog, he left the ground, leaping directly into its neck and knocking it over.

The dog was up immediately and running out through the gate. Elvis chased after him for a few yards, and then came back to Whoopi, just as I arrived. I sat on the ground and held her in my lap. She was shaking and Elvis licked her face. Everything had happened so fast and the big dog had left so quickly that I was never sure whether Elvis had bitten him or had tried to bite him or had just head butted him.

A minute later, Mozart trotted over to us. "What's going on?" he asked.

"Elvis rescued me from a huge dog," said Whoopi.

"Yeah, right. I don't see any huge dog. What really happened, Dad?"

"Exactly that. A big dog pushed the gate open and was intimidating Whoopi. Elvis laid a whack on him that any linebacker would be proud of. You don't see the dog around here because he didn't want any more of Elvis."

"Well, well, my kid brother to the rescue. I knew you had it in you, Elvis. I'm proud of you. You can have one of my squeaky toys to destroy when we get home."

"I think when Mom and I go shopping later, we'll come home with new squeaky toys for everyone in honor of Elvis."

Elvis hadn't said a word all this time. He just kept licking Whoopi.

Elvis is our dog, but he is Whoopi's hero. For the rest of the weekend, she followed Elvis everywhere. I could hear her singing "The Wind Beneath My Wings."

"Did you ever know, you were my hero..."

Elvis loved every minute of it.

PART THREE

LIFE ON THE LAKE

PATRICK M. SHERIDAN

CHAPTER EIGHT

That summer we had a dog door put in. It was inserted into the door leading to the deck and it was just big enough for the dogs to climb or jump through. After the carpenter left, the dogs gathered around.

"What's this?" asked Elvis.

"It's a dog door."

"We don't need a dog door," said Mozart. "We have a door man."

They all thought this was funny.

"Well, now you can go through the door even when your door man is not home."

"How does it work?" asked Whoopi.

"I'll show you," I said. I went out on the deck, leaned over, and pushed the dog door in and out. Diane picked the dogs up one at a time and showed them how to put their front paws on the door; then she guided them through. I caught them on the other side.

"This is really cool," said Whoopi, as she went through the door a couple of times on her own.

Mozart showed us he could do it too, then he said, "There, see, I can do it. It's no big deal. Now, if it's all the same to you, I'll stick with the way nature intended things. I'll let you know when I'm ready to go out and you can come and hold the big door open for me."

Elvis was still struggling with the whole idea of the dog door when Diane had an idea. She took a Puppy Pepperoni outside and held the dog door open so Elvis could see her put it on the ground. He climbed through in a flash, no more questions asked.

Life immediately became more exciting. In the past, when ducks were spotted sitting on our pier, the whispered call of "Ducks!" had sent all of us scrambling for the door. Diane or I had opened the door and the dogs ran down the steps, but there was never much of a chase. Once the door opened, the ducks heard it and jumped off the pier into the water.

The day after the installation, Whoopi looked out the window, saw the ducks, and immediately hit the dog door at a dead run. By the time Mozart and Elvis got to the window and looked down, Whoopi was racing down the steps. As they watched, she got within five feet of the ducks before they jumped into the water.

Time and time again, they leapt through the dog door until they were so exhausted that I made three trips to carry each one of them up the stairs to the bedroom. None of the dogs would ever again have to wait for me to open the door.

"That was great, we almost had them, Dad," said Elvis, giving my face a rare lick.

"I saw that, Elvis. Now are you glad I got a dog door?"

"Yeah, it's really cool. Thanks, Dad."

Later, I saw Mozart standing at the window, looking down at the pier. "What's up Mozart?" I asked.

"I want to see the ducks before Whoopi does, so that I can use my superior tracking skills to sneak up on them and catch them before she scares them off again."

"Superior tracking skills? Mozart, the steps only lead to the pier and the pier is a dead end. Even my tracking skills could find them. The tough part is catching them."

"OK, I meant superior hunting skills. They must have heard Whoopi coming down the stairs. They won't hear me and I'll be all over them before they know it."

"You don't think they'll hear you? You weigh twice as much as Whoopi."

"Oh, great. After we got the twins, you finally stopped with the short jokes and now you're starting with the fat jokes. I'm calling Jenny Craig in the morning."

None of the dogs would ever come closer than five feet to the ducks on the pier—even though the ducks would always wait until the last second to jump. My three hunters were not discouraged. They never stopped believing that the next trip would bring success.

Not long after the dog door went in, Mozart actually did come close to catching a duck, but he doesn't like to talk about it...There is a bank of rocks about four feet wide between the water's edge and the steep rise to the house. Since no one ever walked on the rocks, I had forgotten they were there. One day I carried Mozart outside and set him at the foot of the steps. As we started to walk onto the pier, he noticed a duck sitting on the rocks, about three feet away, facing the water. He whispered that it was the same duck that had needled him through the window the time we had left him home alone. He had previously pointed this duck out to me.

I noticed for the first time that it was possible for Mozart to fit under the railing and to go up onto the rocks. I had never noticed this before because there had never been anything there to attract him.

"Now, I've got you," crowed Mozart as he sped toward the duck. As he came within a few inches, the duck sprang forward and Mozart jumped after him. "You're toast!" he yelled before splashing into the water. "What the hell? Hey, Dad, what's this all about?" he asked, as he paddled furiously.

"It's only water. You've seen the ducks in it. You've been in water when Mom has given you a bath."

"That only came up to my belly and I didn't like that either. What happened to the ground? It gets even deeper when I stop running."

"It's called dog-paddling and you're pretty good at it for a first-timer. I'm actually quite surprised and very proud. I didn't know you could swim."

"Well, I don't want to swim. I really hate it. How do I get out?"

"You could paddle back to the rocks and walk out, but if you paddle over here to me, I'll pull you out."

By now, a crowd had gathered. Whoopi and Elvis were fascinated. Diane was aghast. The ducks were in stitches. And the catfish didn't know what all the commotion was about but they were sure something good would fall to the bottom, so they all circled below.

I set Mozart on the pier. He shook himself off. Then he rolled.

"This pier never felt so good," he said.

"Whoopi and Elvis, do either of you want to see what it is like?" I asked.

"No thanks," chuckled Whoopi. "I just saw what it was like. Thanks for the demonstration, Mozart."

"Never, Dad," said Elvis. "Not in a million years."

A few weeks later, when we were feeding the fish, Whoopi leaned too far over the pier and fell in. I pulled her out immediately. She looked right at Mozart. "Don't say a word. Not one word, or you will experience serious regret." Mozart was rolling on the deck, laughing, but he did not say a word.

We all loved going for rides on the pontoon. As we rode, the dogs sat on the seat with Diane, or on my lap, as Whoopi often did. Sometimes, they sat at the front edge of the pontoon and looked down into the water. We motored towards the ducks, but never got very close to them. Since it was a small, 135-acre lake, it only took a few minutes to go across and back, but it was a real treat.

When moored, the pontoon floor was level with the pier, so it was very easy to walk directly onto the pontoon. If the pontoon drifted, it never slipped more than 10 inches away. About a month after Whoopi went into the water, we were all heading down for a ride on the lake. Elvis was very excited, as usual, and was talking to Whoopi as we stepped onto the boat. "I'm going to sit up front," he said, "and see how many catfish I can..." SPLASH. He had missed the pontoon entirely.

"Dad, Elvis fell in."

"I heard."

I pulled him up. He shook himself dry.

"Should we get a crossing guard next time?" asked Mozart.

"At least, I didn't jump in thinking I could catch a duck."

Now they all knew they could swim. It didn't matter. None of them ever went into the lake again.

CHAPTER NINE

We all loved summer. There was still two hours of daylight left when I came home from work. One night in July, we were on the pier feeding the ducks as we usually did. Over time, we had witnessed a number of changes.

"Dad, drop some bread just off the edge of the pier. Let's see if they'll come right up to the pier," said Whoopi.

"Why? So you can lean over too far and fall in again?"

"*Wow*. Did you see that?" cried Elvis.

"What?" we all asked at once.

"A catfish knocked that duck out of the way and took the bread."

"Elvis, you've been in the sun too long," said Mozart.

"Did the duck dive under for the bread?" asked Whoopi.

"No, the catfish came right up to the top."

"Well, Elvis, I've never seen a catfish do that, but I'll throw some more bread and we'll see if he does it again."

And he did. Then other catfish came to the top, bumping ducks aside, in order to get to the bread first. The splashing caused by the ducks as they were knocked aside by the catfish caused the dogs to laugh hysterically and start to talk all at once.

"Man, that is so cool. Now, *that's entertainment*."

"Look at that fish ram into that duck. Here he comes again, ramming speed coming up."

"Do you think the ducks will launch a counterattack?"

"I'll bet the ducks don't get another piece of bread."

"Sure they will. Look at them *now*. They're moving faster toward the bread while it's still in the air. The fish can't see it until it hits the water."

"We should sell tickets and allow wagering."

"Can we do that?"

"I'm not sure, Whoopi. I know people can gamble on the Ohio River. I believe only dogs can gamble on Lake Clearwater."

Mozart was really getting into it. "Hey, Dad, throw a piece as far as possible from any duck and let's see who gets to it first."

I did and just as three ducks converged on it, a catfish swam up and grabbed it. After the catfish won a few more races, things changed. The ducks started flying to the bread, getting there first, finally. It was starting to get dark.

"Okay, let's go in. Mozart, I'll carry you up first."

"Thanks. This has been great...like biscuits and gravy."

Whoopi beat me up the stairs as I carried Elvis. "I couldn't help but hear Mozart mention biscuits and gravy. Can I have some too?" asked Elvis.

"Sorry, Elvis, it's just an expression. It means you think something is really cool."

"Well, I wish he'd use expressions that don't get a hungry dog's hopes up so much."

"Mom has dinner ready for you guys. To celebrate the Revolution of the Catfish, I'll make bottle-cap sundaes for everybody."

The dogs all spend a great deal of time with Diane, separately and as a pack. She is their caregiver in every sense of the word. If they have a problem, she is the one they go to. Her relationship with each is very close and unique. If she had a favorite, it would be Mozart, since they have been together the longest. She caters to him more than she does the twins. He's a picky eater, doesn't like anything new, and his appetite comes and goes. Eating is rarely important enough for him to make the trip to the kitchen, so he often gets served breakfast in the living room or the bedroom or wherever he happens to be. Yes, he even gets breakfast in bed from time to time.

Mozart is crazy about Diane as well. When she sits on the couch or takes a nap, he always gets the spot next to her and the twins don't challenge him. When she gets dressed up to go out, he gives her his favorite compliment: Hubba, hubba.

"What's Mozart saying?"

"He just said, '*Hubba, hubba.*' Apparently, he thinks you're some dish."

"You sure are, Mom. *Hubba, hubba,* indeed."

Living on a lake can have its downsides. During most summers, we had about a dozen yellow jackets—bees—on our deck. They constantly buzzed around us, and it seemed that if I killed one, two more would appear. One day when I was at work, a yellow jacket stung Mozart on the nose. He went running in to Diane.

"Mozart, what happened?"

"I don't know. One minute I'm playing tag with this bee, and the next, he tags me with his stinger and it hurts really bad."

"It looks terrible. I'll call the vet and see if I should just put ointment on it or if we need to do something more."

"I don't think the bee understood the game. I play tag with Elvis and Whoopi all the time and getting tagged never hurt like this before."

Mozart looked like Cyranno DeBergerac when I got home from work. I asked what happened. He said, "I was stung by a bee. How do I look?"

"You've looked better. How do you feel?"

"It still hurts, but not as bad as it did. Mom put some cream on it and gave me some medicine and it began to feel better. She's the best, isn't she Dad?"

"No argument here, Mozart."

"Hey, Dad, I have an idea. I've been trying to teach the bees how to play tag with me. I chase them and bark like crazy, but all they do is buzz and sting me on the nose. So, I'm thinking, maybe you can come out and teach them how to tag without stinging."

"Thanks for the idea, Mozart, but I'll pass before they sting *me* on the nose. It would be unproductive, and I sure don't want to look like you. No offense."

"None taken. The bees aren't too bright, are they?"

"No, Moz, they aren't"

"But they sure do pack a punch."

"I'll just have to take your word for it. I'm off tomorrow and we'll take the punch out of them. In the meantime, would a bottle-cap sundae help you get some sleep?"

"That would be great. Almost makes it worth it... *As if.*" Malibu Moz liked doing his Valley Girl impression.

The dogs couldn't get enough of the ducks. Once in a while, I took the dogs to the White River where hundreds of ducks sat along the banks.

"It's such a beautiful day. Let's go to the river."

"OK, Mozart, good idea. I'll grab the leashes."

"I was thinking…we probably don't need the leashes anymore. We are pretty well trained now."

"Yeah, right, Moz. You cause those ducks at the river enough trouble as it is."

"I'll just casually walk up to them and ask how they're doing…"

"Mozart, you have never casually walked up to anyone. You even run at Mom and me—barking all the way—when we come home to you."

At the river, I hooked them onto the triple leash, and we started to walk. The ducks watched us coming. We got within ten or twenty yards before they walked to the river and jumped in. Meanwhile, all three dogs were straining at the leash. I strained to hold them back. Every once in a while, some of the ducks failed to see us coming until we got about ten yards away and the dogs started barking and racing toward them. We never came close to catching any.

On the ride home, Whoopi always thanked me for the outing and always told me how pretty she thought the ducks were. The rest of the ride was full of adventure stories by the "boys."

"I can't wait to tell Mom that I almost caught that big white duck, the one that was bigger than me. You'll back me up on that, won't you, Dad?"

"Of course, Elvis. I'll tell her you were the White River Terminator."

He looked forward to getting a hug from Diane and sat back and smiled.

"I could have caught dozens of them if you hadn't held me back on the leash," said Mozart.

"Mozart, you're getting middle-aged. I just might have saved you from the embarrassment of catching them and seeing what they would do to you."

"Oh, great. I finally hear every last short joke you can think of and now you are starting in on the *old dog* jokes."

We all laughed.

"Are you laughing at me?"

"No, Mozart. We're laughing near you. But you are pretty funny."

He went into his Joe Pesci routine: "Do I amuse you? Do you think I'm funny?"

We all laughed even harder.

Mozart, Whoopi, and Elvis actually love all kinds of birds and animals with the possible exception of Canadian geese. Every once in a while, about a dozen geese came to the lake. While they were outnumbered by ducks and catfish, they had such long necks that they easily got more than their fair share of the bread I threw on the lake each evening. Mozart was irked by their unfair advantage.

"Hey, Dad, the geese are getting too much bread. Some of my duck pals aren't getting any."

"The ducks are now your pals?"

"Compared to these honkers, they sure are. I'm going to change the odds."

He started barking at the geese, getting as close to them as he could, by standing at the very edge of the pier. The closest goose was only about three feet away when the others decided to join him. They inched closer and closer, hissing at Mozart. His bark got even louder, which I hadn't thought possible. Then he went into his best Robert De Niro routine: "Are you looking at me? Yeah, that's right. I'm bad. You want a piece of me? Me and my guys are here to protect our ducks."

Now they were *his ducks*.

One of his "guys," Whoopi, was nearly standing on my feet to make sure I didn't leave the dock without her. She wanted no part of Mozart's macho routine.

The geese were just a few inches from Mozart when I decided that they were close enough. "Mozart, that's enough," I said, as I walked towards him.

"Dad, I got this. If one comes up on the pier, his goose will be cooked, if you get my meaning."

"I get your meaning. But I think there is another way to help your new friends."

"Are you taking their side?"

"Not at all. I have an idea. I'll throw the bread just a few inches from each duck so they will get it before the geese can react. We'll neutralize their long-neck advantage."

"Great idea, Dad. That should tick them off...I could have taken them, you know."

"I don't doubt it, Mozart. But then, I'd spend the rest of the night sweeping goose feathers off the pier."

"You got that right."

Elvis was looking at the water where the bread was landing, trying to determine if he could still swim and if the risk was too high to jump in after it. Whenever I saw that look, I dropped a slice next to him. He gulped it down in two bites.

"Ah, worth the wait," he said.

"Patience is its own reward, Elvis."

"I prefer patience and a slice of bread. What was all the commotion?"

Whoopi answered him. "Mozart has decided to become the champion of the ducks, and he tried to take on all the geese."

"No kidding...Hey, Moz, did you show them your De Niro routine you've been practicing in front of the mirror?"

"Of course."

"Were they impressed?"

"Do you even have to ask? You didn't see any geese up here on the dock did you?"

That night when Whoopi and Elvis had already fallen asleep, Mozart was sitting on my lap in bed. "Were you really worried about me getting into it with the geese on the pier?"

"A little, Mozart. I wasn't too worried, because I was there. But you have to be careful when you act aggressively. You could get hurt."

"I suppose you are right, Dad."

"You know, Mozart, a dog has got to know his limitations."

"Now you're quoting Dirty Harry, bad grammar and all."

"Thus endeth the lesson. Would you guys all like bottle-cap sundaes?"

I don't know how dogs understand words, especially when they are asleep—but the twins immediately awoke. All of our days together ended on a high note but those with bottle-cap sundaes were still the best.

CHAPTER TEN

While we enjoyed living on the lake, we never went into the water, even though the water was so clean and clear we could see through it to the bottom. Diane and I just didn't have any more interest in being in the water than the dogs did. The only exception to this was the one weekend a year when my brother Tim and his wife Marian brought their family to visit; they virtually spent their entire visit in the lake.

For the dogs, it was a barking holiday. The kids raced down the pier with the dogs running full speed behind them, thinking they wanted to play. At the end of the pier, the kids jumped off and the dogs came to a screeching halt. Two things fascinated me about this ritual. First, I hadn't thought that dogs could come to a screeching halt—but they can—and every time it happened, I was sure they had run too hard to the pier's end and that this time they would go over the edge. But they never did. Not in all the summers they played this game. Second, I could never understand why the dogs never figured out that every single run was destined to end the same way.

"Mozart, you have been running and barking after Gavin and Ryan and Paul for an hour. What are you trying to accomplish?"

"When they start running, I think they want to play with me."

"Have you noticed that they *always* run to the end of the pier?"

"Yes, I have."

"What do they do when they reach the end of the pier?"

"Well, so far, they have been jumping in the water."

"*So far?* What else is there to do at the end of the pier?"

"They haven't figured that out yet. But when they do, I'll be there and ready to play."

"Has it occurred to you that they *have* figured it out and all they ever want to do is jump into the water?"

"There is that possibility. But what fun would that be?"

"Well, it's fun for those who enjoy swimming. You can swim. Why don't you just jump in and join them?"

"Been there. Done that. No, thanks, never again."

"Elvis, why have you been running and barking at the kids all morning?"

51

"Because I think Mozart is on to something. He usually is. When he runs and barks it usually means he is getting close."

"Well, this time it simply means he's getting a good workout."

"Whoopi, what are you doing?"

"I'm just watching Bridget and Maureen. They float on top of the water without paddling at all. Not even the ducks do that."

"They are floating on rafts. *We can do that.* I'll put my bathing suit on and get in the canoe. You and Elvis and Mozart can get in with me and we'll float out there with the girls."

I emerged from the house in my bathing suit. I have always been overweight and while they make bathing suits in my size—I just don't look good in them. The dogs get a big kick out of this.

"Looking good," laughed Mozart. "I wish I could remember some of those fat jokes the comics tell on TV. I don't think I should be hearing any more jokes from you for the rest of the summer..."

"I forgot you wore that suit last summer. I can see why you only break it out for about ten minutes a year," said Elvis.

Even my little Whoopi, who adores me, joined in. "Let's get this over with as fast as possible. If any of the neighbors see you in that I'll be mortified."

"All right, all right. I know I'm overweight. But I'm not the fattest guy in town."

"No, just the fattest guy willing to be seen wearing that bathing suit," says Mozart. They all laughed.

I got in the canoe. Diane put Mozart and Elvis in with me. Whoopi was long-gone. I don't know if she feared the canoe would tip over or sink with me in it or if she just didn't want to be seen on the lake with me in that bathing suit, but she completely disappeared.

Until that day, I had only seen three expressions on Mozart's face. One was his very sorrowful look. We call it his Conway Twitty look, since we first noticed it the day that Conway Twitty died. The second was his ear-to-ear grin with his tongue hanging out, normally seen when he is playing or has been running. The third was his "What am I thinking now?" look, which is his most serious and is usually seen when he all-too-frequently stares at me until I stop what I'm doing to figure out what he wants.

Obviously, I had hoped for his ear-to-ear grin and could have lived with his "What am I thinking now?" look and naturally expected to avoid the Conway Twitty died expression. What I saw was a look of terror.

"What's up, Mozart?"

"What's up is that you don't know the first thing about paddling a canoe, do you?"

"What's to know? I'll just paddle around for a while, then we'll head back to the dock."

"Yeah right. We'll probably drift off to the middle of the lake. Can you even swim?"

"Not that well, but I'm wearing a life preserver."

"No kidding. Well, we can't swim well either and we aren't wearing life preservers."

"We're not going to tip over, and we're just a few feet from the pier. Relax and enjoy the ride."

"The possibility of simply tipping over is not what is really bothering me."

"Well, what is bothering you, Mozart?"

"You weigh 230 pounds and you are at that end of the canoe, and Elvis and I together weigh 50 pounds and we are at this end of the canoe. If you tip over backwards, I'm afraid you'll catapult us through the air all the way to 82nd Street."

It was a funny image, but he wasn't even smiling.

"Okay, we'll head back to the pier. How are you doing, Elvis?"

Elvis was in a fetal position. While Whoopi sleeps in a fetal position, Elvis had never rolled himself into one, until now. "Are we done having fun?" he asked. "I just want to get back on the pier…"

We pulled up to the pier and Diane lifted each of them out of the canoe. I started to climb up the ladder. When my face got just above the pier, it was nose to nose with Mozart, who was standing there waiting for me.

"I know you meant well, but that was the worst ten minutes of my life."

"I understand, Mozart. Sorry about that."

"I would never threaten you, Dad. But if you promise never to take me in the canoe again, this urge I have to go pee on your pillow might just go away…"

Elvis was laying down hugging the dock.

"I promise," I said.   Just then, Whoopi came running down the steps to the pier.

Mozart and Elvis were immediately all over her.

"Boy, did you miss it."

"It was great! You should have been there."

"That was the most fun we've had in years. You'll have to go with Dad next time."

Whoopi looked at me and winked. She wasn't buying any of it.

PART FOUR

WINTER GAMES

PATRICK M. SHERIDAN

CHAPTER ELEVEN

The first time the twins saw it snow, they were fascinated. They sat by the window and watched as their world changed. By the time I got home from work, the snow was about three inches deep.

"What's going on outside?" asked Whoopi.

"It's just snowing. Snow is soft, feels cool. Some people like to play in it."

"Can we play in it?"

"Sure, Elvis. Let me get my coat."

I opened the door and Mozart ran right out. He had been in snow before and liked to run in it. Whoopi was hesitant. She was so small that, if it kept snowing, the snow would be too deep for her. Elvis waited a minute or so more before joining Whoopi and me on the deck. Mozart was already having a ball.

"Hey, Dad, are you going to build another one of your pitiful snowmen this year?"

"Mozart, what's a snowman?" asked Elvis.

"It's supposed to be a man made of snow," laughed Mozart. "But the way Dad builds it, it looks more like three balls stacked on top of each other with a hat on the top."

"I thought my snowman looked pretty good last year."

"It looked like Jabba the Hut. The arms kept falling off. The wind blew the hat away. But I loved the 'What me worry?' look you put on its face with black buttons."

"Do you guys want to see me build a snowman?"

"Yeah!" said the twins.

"Nothing is ever as bad as Mozart says it is," added Elvis.

I started making the snowman. For the base, I made a ball as large as I could roll. (This cleared a path for the dogs to run through and they loved it.) For the middle, I rolled a ball as big as I could lift. (I could never have lifted the first.) The third ball of snow was the smallest, about size 7½ for the head. I put a baseball cap on it, did my black-button thing for its face, and stood back to admire my work.

Mozart was right. The snowman did look like Jabba the Hut from the *Star Wars* movie. It was an enormous round pyramid and looked very ugly.

The dogs get a certain look when they've run for a long time and are completely winded. They had that look. Their tongues hung out and they were grinning from ear to ear. They were trying hard not to laugh and kept looking down as if to muffle their giggles.

"Well, did I call it or not?" asked Mozart.

"I never would have believed it," said Elvis.

Whoopi tried to be tactful. "Dad probably grew up in the South and never saw snow when he was a kid. Right, Dad?"

"No, Whoopi. I grew up in Detroit."

"Ouch," said Elvis.

"It's a good thing that you don't work with your hands, Dad," said Mozart.

And then they all lost it. Even I had to laugh.

"Let's go get Mom," said Whoopi, as she ran through the dog door with the others close behind.

Diane said it was the worst-looking snowman she'd ever seen.

I left it standing, as a continuing source of amusement for us all. The sun, finally, mercifully, melted it away.

CHAPTER TWELVE

Since we stayed indoors most days during the winter, we spent a lot of time playing with "dog toys." These were toys intended for kids, but we found ways to enjoy them that most children would never think of.

The best toys for our dogs are those that can fly, make noise, and are chewable. If we found a toy that had two of these characteristics, it was like hitting a home run. Finding a toy that did all three was even better—and we did find a few.

Whenever we came home from the store, Mozart, Whoopi, and Elvis would be waiting at the door. "Hi, Dad! Did you buy a toy for us?"

"Mozart, why would I buy you guys a toy? Is it somebody's birthday?"

"No, but it's freezing outside, and since we can't go out to play, we'd all love to play inside with *you*."

"Well, go get one of your squeaky toys or stuffed animals that you haven't already chewed your way through."

"Dad, we played with those old toys while you were gone just to remind us of how great it would be when you came home to play with us."

"It looks like Elvis still likes the old toys."

Elvis could pull the stuffing out of a stuffed animal long after you thought there wasn't any stuffing left. Then he slept on the empty carcass.

"Dad, you know Elvis will play with anything. However, a new toy would sure pep all of us up."

Whoopi walked over. "Did you bring *me* anything, Dad?"

"Actually, I did come across something you might find amusing. It's a stomp rocket that shoots nerf arrows, so we can use it in the house."

As I took it out of the bag, Elvis ran over and all three dogs began to jump up and down and bark. Their tails wagged a mile a minute. I put the nerf arrow on the rocket and aimed it toward the far end of the room. When I stomped on the rocket the arrow flew the length of the living room, hit the wall, and fell to the floor. The dogs raced after it.

Mozart arrived first, bit into the arrow's rubbery, soft foam, put his foot on it, and broke it in half. Elvis arrived a second later and picked up the half, ran into a corner and started biting it into smaller pieces. Whoopi watched as they ripped the arrow to shreds, then came back to me.

"As I was asking, did you get anything for me?"

"Well, Whoopi, I clearly underestimated the life span of a nerf arrow. Fortunately, three came with the rocket and I bought a few packs of refills. I'll shoot another one."

I loaded and shot another arrow into the next room, away from Mozart and Elvis. No sooner had my foot stomped the rocket, then the two left the pieces of shredded arrow to race through the door after the new one. But this time, Whoopi got there first, grabbed it, and ran under the couch. Mozart and Elvis were too big to follow her there.

"Dad, tell Whoopi to come out and share the toy, like I did with Elvis."

"Mozart, you didn't share anything with Elvis. He got there before you could eat the whole thing and he took half while you were busy."

"Well, if you want to nit-pick, you could say that, but Whoopi has a whole one and Elvis and I had to split one."

Meanwhile, Elvis was trying to coax Whoopi out from under the couch. "If you come out with the arrow, you can have half of my dinner tonight when you've finished yours."

Whoopi started to laugh and almost choked on the arrow. "Elvis, you always finish your dinner before I can take my second bite. Even if you could remember such a promise you could never keep it."

I took out the third arrow and Elvis ran over and waited with Mozart. It occurred to me that if I could get to the arrow before they did, I might finally shoot the same arrow more than once. I stomped and we all raced down the hall. Mozart got to the arrow first and had it between his teeth, but I pulled on it before he could use his foot for leverage and break it. We were in a standoff. Elvis immediately bit the other end. Now the standoff was three-way. They each had an end and I held the middle. Nobody moved. I let go and they each stood their ground. Nobody moved. I got down on the floor and bit the arrow in the middle.

Through gritted teeth, Mozart asked, "What are you doing?"

Without opening my mouth, I mumbled, "Trying to get my arrow back so I can shoot it again."

"I got it first. You and Elvis should let go. Possession is 9/10ths of the law."

"So, now you have a law degree. I'm glad you have it because you don't have possession of this arrow."

Elvis said, "You got that right. Besides, you only have the tip end, Mozart. I have the bigger end."

"Well, if I could make a suggestion…You and Elvis let go, and I'll shoot it again."

"No thanks," said Mozart. "I can outlast both you and Elvis.

Elvis said, "I just want to chew something. I'll be happy with the end I have."

Diane walked in and couldn't believe what she saw—her husband on the floor with two of her dogs, all with an arrow, the same arrow, in their mouths. She went for the camera. Meanwhile, Whoopi had finished destroying her arrow and came out from under the couch. If our arrow had been about four inches longer, Whoopi would have been able to join in.

Diane took the photo. Eventually, Diane would show this photo to just about everyone we knew.

"You guys have outlasted me," I said as I let go. Mozart and Elvis stared at each other over the arrow for another few minutes.

"I'll split it with you," said Mozart.

"Deal," said Elvis. They broke the arrow in half and tore into it.

Over many winters, the stomp rocket remained one of our favorite toys, despite the fact that I never did figure out how to make an arrow last longer than a few minutes.

The best toy ever made, according to Mozart, was nerf football. It was shot from a gun with a loud bang. Mozart liked to chase it and eat the nerf off. About three inches of the spongy material covered the ball's hard plastic center. After only a bite or two, I'd catch him and use the same ball to take another shot. Unlike a nerf arrow, a nerf football could be used for a dozen shots before Mozart had chewed off all the nerf. Once the nerf was gone, he'd chew through the hard plastic. I ordered boxes of refills direct from the company, but eventually the company stopped making them and I ran out of refills.

"This is the last football, Mozart. Should we save it?"

"No, let's go for it. Let her rip."

We played for about ten minutes. I ran as fast as I could so I could make it last. When he finally bit through the plastic, it wouldn't shoot anymore and he was completely winded.

"That's it, Mozart. You've eaten the last nerf football in America."

"That was great. Thanks, Dad."

"I wish the company hadn't gone out of business and I could get more. Sorry partner."

"Don't worry about it. The memories will last a lifetime."

CHAPTER THIRTEEN

Hundreds of books have been written on the subject of how to train dogs—behaviors you should expect and things you should or should not do. I have scanned a few. Diane has read several—but when it comes to our dogs, her heart usually overrides her head.

Mozart, on the other hand, claims to have read all of these books. He can quote them verbatim and is always available as a resource, whenever the need arises.

"How's dinner?"

"Fine thanks, Mozart."

"What are you eating?"

"A hamburger."

"Great! I love hamburger. You are going to share it with your favorite dog, right?"

"You know you're not supposed to eat at the table, Mozart."

"*What?* Where did you ever hear such nonsense?"

"It's in some dog book. Dogs aren't supposed to eat at the table."

"You misread it. It says dogs aren't supposed to eat on the table. That's no problem. I won't eat on the table. Just throw me a piece of your hamburger and I'll eat it down here."

"You think you're pretty funny, don't you?"

"Absolutely. So, do I get some hamburger for making you laugh?"

That's how it started. With time it got worse. After we got Whoopi and Elvis, he became the dog book expert for the group. One night when I brought cookies to bed, all three dogs were on my lap immediately.

"What are those?" asked Elvis.

"Cookies."

"Can we have some?"

"You guys ate not too long ago. You can't be hungry."

"But we didn't eat cookies."

"Yeah...Don't you want us to experience all of life's pleasures?" rejoined Whoopi.

"Cookies aren't good for you."

I had stated it as a fact, and with that, Whoopi and Elvis had looked at Mozart. On cue, he went into his act.

"Dad, Dad, Dad...Where do you get this information?"

"The dog books say it could make you sick."

"You have to read the whole chapter, Dad. It says 'if eaten on an empty stomach' cookies could possibly make you sick. However, as you just reminded Elvis, we just recently ate. So, it won't be a problem for us if you give us some of your cookies."

I started to grin and they knew Mozart had done it again.

He decided to press his luck. "In fact, if you are still concerned about it, you could feed us some cheese. Since cheese is binding, it will offset the remote possibility of any problem posed by the cookies."

The very notion of solving a potential food problem with an additional food product was too much for the twins. Whoopi immediately turned her back to me so that I wouldn't see her laughing. Elvis started to drool and wagged his tail furiously.

They all got cookies, which they loved. They all also got cheese, which they loved as well.

Later, as I was trying to get to sleep, I could hear them whispering to each other.

"Do you ever worry that Dad will read the dog books and catch on to you?" asked Whoopi.

"No. It's actually an old, Dad trick. Kelly says that when she was a little girl he pulled this trick on her all the time. No matter what question she asked, he made up an answer. Kelly said it took years for her to catch on to him."

"So you're hoping it will take him years to catch on to you?" asked Whoopi.

Mozart just smiled and said, "No. He knows the game. He just loves to see it played."

"You really outdid yourself tonight," said Whoopi.

"Yeah," said Elvis. "It's a good thing you remember all them books you read."

Mozart laughed. "Elvis, dogs can't read. Not even me."

Elvis stared at Mozart with a puzzled look. "What do you mean, you can't read?"

My next door neighbor owned a very large female Akita named Tojo. She was well behaved and very quiet. My dogs thought there was something wrong with her.

"Dad, what's the matter with Tojo? Why doesn't she ever bark?"

"She's been trained not to bark, Mozart. Many people find dog barking annoying."

"Do you find us annoying?" asked Whoopi.

"Perish the thought. But when the neighbors are outside, we prefer you do your barking inside our house."

Elvis said, "I once saw Tojo in the lake last summer and she didn't even trip or fall in. She just *jumped* in. What's wrong with her?"

"Nothing, Elvis. Dogs are natural swimmers, as all you guys found out the hard way. Many dogs even enjoy it."

They all laughed. "That's a good one, Dad," said Elvis.

When we were out for a walk, we often saw Tojo through the gate in her courtyard. All three dogs would start barking, but Mozart was obsessed. He was determined to meet Tojo.

Our properties had similar decks and courtyards separated by a solid wood fence that seemed more like a wall. Mozart loved to run to the edge of our deck, stick his head through the fence that faced the lake, and peek around the wall in an effort to see Tojo's side. In seven years, he only saw Tojo up close one time. I just happened to be leaning over the railing when Mozart and Tojo both stuck their heads through the fence at the same time and found themselves nose to nose. Mozart went ballistic. It was the closest he had been to another dog, other than the twins, since his notorious trip to the kennel years before. Tojo retreated. Mozart started to chew on the wall.

"Hey, Mozart, what are you doing?"

"I'm trying to make a hole in the wall so I can go over to play with Tojo."

"What makes you think Tojo wants to play with you? She outweighs you by 85 pounds. Is she going to juggle you?"

"Very funny. I'll charm the socks off of her."

"Those aren't socks. She just has very hairy feet."

"Well, she's all female, and there is more of her than any female I've ever seen."

"I understand. But, you can't eat the wall. Let's go in."

I picked him up and carried him inside the house. Later that night, when he was sitting on my lap, I said, "You had a pretty exciting day."

"I can't believe I finally met Tojo…It was a moment that will live in my heart forever."

"Well, don't eat the wall anymore. I think there is concrete behind the wood, so you can't get through anyway. Just out of curiosity, what would you have done if you had been able to get into her yard?"

His eyes glazed over, as he said, "I would have shown her a time she would never forget."

I considered reminding him that he had been neutered, but didn't want to ruin his reverie. He went to sleep that night with a big grin on his face. It was still there when I woke early for work the next morning.

Mozart, Whoopi, and Elvis believed any sound they heard was an intruder and frequently jumped on and off the couch and ran up and down the stairs. Worst of all, they jumped off the bed, which was too high.

Dachshunds have long backs and short legs and are susceptible to back injuries. Ours were no exception. We decided to make it easier for them to get down from the bed, and if possible, enable them to get up onto the bed without being picked up. We bought a two-step staircase.

"What's that?" they all shouted when I set it next to the bed.

"It's steps. Just like on the front porch and leading down to the pier."

"Cool," said Whoopi as she ran up the steps onto the bed.

"Why don't you just pick us up and put us on the bed like you always do?" asked Elvis.

"I'll still pick you up, most of the time, Elvis. I got this, primarily, so you could go down the steps and save wear and tear on your back."

It took a while, but eventually they all used the steps. Occasionally they jumped off the bed when they were really excited, but jumping down became less usual when they began to compare the result of running down the steps with the impact they felt on their backs when they jumped.

It occurred to Diane and me that we had clearly spoiled our dogs. We didn't care. What might be a minor inconvenience to us could be a significant benefit to them. In return, all three dogs gave us their total loyalty and affection. We had fun with them every single day and we wanted to do whatever we could to make those days last forever.

CHAPTER FOURTEEN

From time to time, when I think of certain characteristics and behaviors that my dogs have, I recall the title of an old Clint Eastwood movie, *The Good, the Bad, and the Ugly.*

The "good" includes some of the most charming traits—loyal, loveable, playful behaviors—that you could ever imagine. Mozart, for example, has more fun than any dog I've ever seen. He plays until he is exhausted, then lies down on the couch next to Diane or me and promptly falls asleep. But even if he has been asleep for only one minute, if I accidentally step on a squeaky toy, he is at my side in a flash—and ready to play again.

"What's up, Dad? Do you want to toss the squeaky toy? I'll chase it..."

"No, Mozart. I just want to get the paper so I can sit next to you and read it."

"Then why did you make the toy squeak?"

"I made the toy squeak because you left it in the middle of the room and I accidentally stepped on it."

"Is this some kind of April Fools' joke? I had just fallen asleep. Couldn't you walk around the toy?"

"Easier said than done, Mozart. It's hard not to step on your toys after you're through playing with them. You leave them all over the floor."

"I thought you liked to put them away as part of your exercise program. I'm only trying to do my part to get you into shape."

"Thanks, Mozart. I can develop my own exercise routine."

As he walked back to the couch to snuggle up with Diane, he mumbled, "Yeah, right, and I'm the halftime entertainment at this year's Super Bowl."

Every night around dusk, Mozart jumped up on the couch in the study, climbed up across its back, then jumped to the window sill where he would sit and wait for me to come home from work. As soon as I turned into the driveway, he ran to the front door. There's not a day that I can remember when he was not at that door to greet me, face grinning, tail wagging—and ready to play.

Michael Doonesbury once wrote that Elizabeth Taylor had "violet eyes to die for." Whoopi's eyes have that same intensity. They can be soft and black or piercing. She uses her eyes to communicate her feelings more than any other animal, or even any person, I've ever known. When she wants your attention, or wants to be held, or just wants to let you know that she is happy that you are home, she will find a way to get as close to your face as possible, then she will look straight into your eyes. If you pick her up, she will cuddle, rolling herself into a ball in your arms. In this position, she can instantly fall asleep.

When Whoopi has done something good, she wants you to know it. At night, I work on the computer. About two hours after Diane and the dogs have gone to sleep, Whoopi gets up to pee. Because the dogs have such short hair and because it gets so cold on winter nights, we lay a newspaper on the floor in the corner of the bathroom. After Whoopi goes on the paper, she appears at my side. Conversations with her at this late hour can be very one-sided.

"I see you looking at me Whoopi. I'm working on the computer."

She continues to sit there, staring at me, not saying a word.

"Whoopi, don't just sit there staring at me. What do you want?"

Finally, I pick her up and she sits on my lap, nose to nose with me.

"I want to show you something," she says.

"I know what you want to show me…You peed on the paper. You do it every night."

Her tail starts to wag as she continues to look directly into my eyes.

"All right…Do you want to show me *where* you peed on the paper?"

Her tail now wags furiously. Her moment of glory is near. I get up and carry her to the bathroom. As expected, she has peed directly on the paper.

"Wow, Whoopi. Congratulations. You peed on the paper. You are such a *good girl*."

She beams. I rub her head, give her a small piece of pepperoni, and carry her back to bed. "I wish you could teach your brothers how to aim at the paper better."

"Dad, if you covered the entire room with newspaper, Elvis would still somehow miss it."

From the day we brought him home, Elvis has been our "family dog." He is happy just being a part of the family and greatly appreciates anything that we do for him. A pat on the head or a kind word puts him on cloud nine for hours. He loves children and, in turn, they always like him best. He has every characteristic you could hope for in a dog. He never causes us any trouble.

Elvis is as happy with a half-destroyed toy that Mozart no longer wants, as Mozart is when he gets a brand new toy.

"Hey, Elvis, how are you doing?"

"I'm doing great. There's still some stuffing left in this teddy bear and I get to be the one to tear it out."

"That's terrific Elvis. It looks like you're doing an excellent job."

"Thanks. If you need anything chewed, just give me a call."

"You got it, Elvis. When it comes to chewing, you're the champion in this household."

He grins from ear to ear, but never stops chewing.

Once we gave him a big Clifford the Big Red Dog. He chewed on it and pulled stuffing out it for almost a year.

Elvis really likes Mozart, but he adores Whoopi. They play together. They take naps together. They even spend a lot of time grooming each other. He goes everywhere she goes and whenever she barks or seems to be in any kind of trouble, he immediately races to her side—even if he is in the middle of eating.

The "bad" in my dogs includes habits probably common to all dogs, but that can take some getting used to.

I often took the dogs for walks through our neighborhood. At first, I tried walking them on three separate leashes, but they constantly went in different directions, and every few steps, I had to stop and untangle myself from the leashes wrapped around my legs. Finally, I purchased one long leash that had three small leashes attached to the end. The dogs could never get more than a few feet from each other and I never again got entangled.

Our walks were usually a reminder that there is nothing too gross for a dog to smell, lick, or roll in. "*Whoopi,* get up! Don't roll on the street. Get off that."

The others turned to see what was up. "Hey, Whoop, what you got there?"

Now they were all sniffing. Suddenly Elvis was upside down, wiggling his back on the asphalt. I pulled the leash to get him up and away. It was a dead worm.

"You guys are gross. Why do you do that?"

Mozart answered, "Dachshunds are hounds. We love new smells. We never smell anything like a dead worm in the house."

"Thank God. And you are not going to find a smell like that in the house either."

"That's where you are wrong. If even one of us can roll around in it, we can carry the smell into the house and keep it there until our next bath...Don't knock it till you try it."

"Never happen. You guys are gross."

In search of the next new smell, we run down the street. "The sense of smell is wasted on humans," says Mozart.

"Word up," agrees Elvis. Elvis had been watching far too much MTV.

Another bad characteristic of dogs is their propensity to pass gas at inappropriate times and places. We often give the dogs baloney, which they really enjoy, but nothing is more deadly than the "baloney farts." These generally come at night.

"Oh man...that is awful. Did you guys have baloney tonight?"

"Yeah, and it was great," says Mozart.

"Well, you guys really are 'the wind beneath my sheets' tonight, and I don't appreciate it."

"To a dog, all smells are fascinating."

"Well, next time, get fascinated away from me."

"Okay," he said. Then he mumbled, "Humans...can't live with them, can't live without them."

"Ugly" consists of dogs imitating sexual activities. At our house, it usually starts with Whoopi on top of Elvis while Elvis is chewing a

71

dog biscuit. We hear it before we see it because Elvis starts growling. He's upset enough to growl, but not upset enough to stop eating.

"Whoopi, stop humping Elvis. What exactly are you trying to do, anyway?"

"This is a natural animal activity, as you well know."

"Not with you on his back—and besides, we had you fixed so it wouldn't be so natural."

Whoopi fell off and Mozart immediately climbed on. Elvis growled even louder. He sounded furious, though still not furious enough to stop eating.

"Mozart, leave him alone. You're not supposed to hump your brother."

"The pickings are kind of slim around here. I have to keep in shape in case I ever meet Tojo."

"Well, you're going to need a stepladder if you ever meet Tojo."

"It will take more than short jokes to throw me off my game when I catch up with her."

Whoopi climbed aboard Mozart, who was still on top of Elvis. Elvis growled really loud now that he had finished eating. He even tried to get his head around to snap at them both.

I said to Diane, "At least we don't have company. No one would believe that we hadn't perverted the dogs."

"But company is coming for Christmas," said Mozart. "That's why we are practicing."

With that, they all fell off Elvis, laughing. Elvis stopped growling and looked around for another biscuit.

"You guys think you're pretty funny, but we better not see any of these x-rated performances when we have guests—or I'll get the crate out of the garage."

"Okay," said Mozart. "We were just messing with you. We'll keep our performances for private viewing only."

"Thanks. One viewing is quite enough for my entire lifetime."

"You just need to lighten up a bit, Dad. We've both seen much worse on Cinemax."

PART FIVE

ON THE ROAD

PATRICK M. SHERIDAN

CHAPTER FIFTEEN

One night, we were all sitting in bed watching TV when Diane and I decided to spring a surprise on the dogs.

"Hey, Dad, why did you turn the TV off? We were watching 'Frasier,' and Eddie—*the dog*—is one of our favorite TV characters."

"Well, Elvis, we have a surprise for you guys."

Whoopi came over and sat on my lap. Mozart lay close to Diane. Elvis sat transfixed at the end of the bed.

"Is your surprise better than seeing Eddie on 'Frasier?'" asked Mozart.

"How would you all like to go to Baltimore with us next week for Christmas?"

"Cool!"…"Wow!"…"This is great." Then came their questions—all at once:

"Is Baltimore where our cousins live?" "How long does it take to get there?" "When will we come back home?"

Diane and I laughed, and I said, "We are all going to take a trip in the RV next week. We are going to Baltimore to see the kids and their families."

"And we are really going with you?'

"Yes, you are, Mozart."

"And staying overnight with you?"

"That's right, Whoopi."

"Where will we sleep? What will we eat? How far is it?" they chorused.

"It will take all day for us to drive there. We will take some food and water, but we'll also stop at some places along the way. We'll stay somewhere that dogs are allowed to stay."

"This is so cool," said Mozart. "Will we meet other dogs there?"

"I hope not, Mozart. But you might."

"This is great. Our first vacation together. What should we pack?"

"Pack your favorite stuffed animals and squeaky toys, and we'll take care of the rest."

Mozart looked at Diane. "You're from Baltimore, right, Mom? Will we get to see where you grew up?"

"Yes, you will, Mozart. And you'll not only see ducks there, but you might also see rabbits and squirrels."

"We've never seen a rabbit or a squirrel. Will they play with us?" asked Whoopi.

"Not if they can help it. But you may get to chase them around a little bit."

Shortly thereafter, we turned out the lights to go to sleep. Mozart and Whoopi did not lie down in their usual spots up near Diane and me. They were down by Elvis, near the foot of the bed, whispering, tails wagging throughout the night. I couldn't hear everything they said, but occasionally I caught a word here or there: "...rabbits... squirrels...RV...motel...Baltimore...cousins...vacation...ducks..."
Then in gleeful, whispery voices, they all started singing the song "Holiday Road" from Chevy Chase's *Vacation* movie. The last thing I heard was "*Holiday Roooooooad...*"

The next morning we picked up the RV and brought it home. We started to load it, but the dogs couldn't wait to see it. "Come on Dad, let us just take a look before you start packing."

"Okay, Moz. Come on guys. Let's go see the RV."

They raced up the two steps leading to the RV's back door. It was a big RV. For about three minutes, they ran wild inside. They ran to the front and jumped on and off the seats. They jumped on the couch and walked back and forth over the cushions, constantly sniffing. They ran under the table, jumped onto its seat, then onto the tabletop. Next, they moved into the bathroom, then the bedroom. I had brought their little steps and they ran up onto the bed, then down, and up again. They never stopped talking the entire time.

"This is so *cool...*"

"Hey, Elvis, look over here."

"Mozart, look what I found..."

"Wait till Mom sees this."

"Whoopi, look under here..."

"Hey Dad, what's this for?"

"Try to catch me up here!"

"Let's get up on the bed..."

"I'm sitting on this chair."

"I'm riding on the bed."

We finished packing and loading dog food, dog toys, dog blankets, and dog pillows and finally managed to pack a few clothes of our own.

Diane drove and I sat in the passenger seat. We weren't even out of the driveway before Whoopi discovered the best seat in the house. She jumped off the couch where I had put all three dogs, jumped into my lap to look out the window, noticed the dashboard and leapt onto it. She crossed back and forth along the RV's enormous windshield, before curling up in the dashboard's left corner directly in front of Diane, below eye level. By then, Mozart had jumped on my lap and was climbing onto the dashboard and Elvis had jumped off the couch, come over, and stood staring up at me. I picked him up and set him on the dashboard with the others. Now all could see the entire horizon.

"Wow...this is beautiful," said Elvis.

"We can see the whole world," said Whoopi.

"These seats are almost perfect, Dad," said Mozart.

"And what would make them perfect, Mozart?"

"We left our blankets on the couch..."

At the next stoplight, I grabbed the three blankets and picked the dogs up one at a time to spread their blankets under them. As Diane turned onto the Interstate, they started singing *"Holiday Rooooooooooad."* Ten minutes later, they were all sound asleep.

We had a great trip. The dogs rode facing the windshield except when I moved from the passenger's seat. When I sat on the couch, they jumped down and joined me. When I took a nap on the bed, they all ran up the dog steps to nap with me. The drive from Indianapolis to Baltimore can be done in one long day. Diane wanted to make the trip in a day and wanted to do all the driving. The dogs and I had nothing better to do than enjoy the scenery.

"This is really great. Where are we now?"

"We are on I-70 in Ohio, Mozart."

"I thought you said we were on I-70 in Indiana."

"We *were* on I-70 in Indiana, but now we are in Ohio."

"It looks like Indiana. I think you're putting us on."

"Well, if you had been awake, you would have seen the sign that read Welcome to Ohio."

"I think you're making that up. This looks exactly like Indiana. You better recheck your map."

"I don't need to recheck my map, Mozart. If you stay awake, you'll see the Ohio-West Virginia border in a couple of hours."

"Did you say we were on I-70 in Indiana and now we are on I-70 in Ohio?" asked Elvis.

"Yes, Elvis. That's right."

"Why did we take I-70 out of Indiana?"

"We didn't, Elvis. I-70 is an Interstate. I-70 runs all the way from Maryland to California."

"Are we going to California? That would be so cool. That's where all the dogs on TV live."

"The TV dogs will have to wait. We're not going to California this trip."

"Could we just stop by for a little while?"

"Elvis, California is 2,000 miles in the opposite direction."

"Well, if you put it to a vote, I vote for going to California."

"Look at your mother gripping the steering wheel. Do you think she'll be taking any votes today?"

Elvis looked at Diane staring at the endless highway ahead of her. "Good point. Baltimore, here we come."

Whoopi jumped from the dashboard to my lap. "I have a question."

"What's that, Whoopi?"

"When are we going to take a break?"

"Good idea. It's almost time for lunch and there is a rest stop in a few miles. We'll get something to eat and stretch our legs there."

We parked at the end of the parking lot, as far away as we could get from the rest of the vehicles and the people. It didn't help. The dogs strained at their leashes and barked at everyone they could see.

We headed toward the dog run. It was near the woods in the back.

"Wow, this is great. This sure doesn't smell like Indiana."

"Elvis, smell this…"

"Mozart, come here, look at this."

"Look what I found, Whoopi."

"Hey, guys, come and roll in this stuff with me."

"No rolling!" I yelled.

"Okay, okay, but this smells better than Indiana."

"Dad, let's move to Ohio. I love the way Ohio smells."

"Mozart, this is a dog run. Every day, hundreds of dogs come here. All of Ohio doesn't smell like this. Not even the Buckeyes."

"What's a Buckeye?" asked Elvis.

"Forget it," said Mozart. "Ohio State beat Notre Dame last fall and Dad still hasn't gotten over it."

I'm not sure they ever lifted their noses more than a quarter-inch off the ground the entire time we were there. Whoopi sighed, "You can bring me here anytime, Dad. This place is the best."

We locked the dogs in the RV, and Diane and I headed towards the restaurant. The dogs ran to the dashboard and barked after us until we were out of sight. They started barking again as soon as they saw us coming back across the parking lot. Diane had ordered extra bacon with her meal so that she could give them a treat. For months after this, anytime they heard the word Ohio it brought a wistful look to their faces.

When we arrived in Baltimore, we stayed at The Residence Inn, which permits pets. The suite had an upstairs. We didn't have stairs in our home and since these stairs were carpeted, we let the dogs spend their first five minutes running up and down the stairway. Then they tired.

"This is so cool," said Elvis. "I like our new house."

"It's only ours for the weekend, Elvis. Then, we are going back home."

"Let's go check out the hood," said Mozart.

Whoopi was already at the door. "Yeah, Dad, come on."

We walked around the various buildings and finally came to the corner of the property designated as the pet area.

"Wow, this place smells great. We're back in Ohio, right, Dad?"

"No, Mozart. It just smells like Ohio because this is where all the people bring their dogs."

"Well, I like it as much as Ohio. This is my favorite motel."

"Ours too," said the twins.

I finally dragged them away, and we went back to our rooms. That night, after we ate, the five of us sat in bed watching TV.

"What do people mean when they say 'It's a dogs life'?" asked Mozart.

"It means they have never spent a day with the three of you," said Diane.

CHAPTER SIXTEEN

As I began to plan for retirement, Diane and I decided that we would move back to Baltimore, which was closer to most of our kids and grandchildren and to all of Diane's other relatives.

In anticipation of taking an early retirement, we went house hunting on one of our Baltimore visits and decided to look out in the country. We wanted to buy some land and have a lot of room to play with the dogs. About 25 miles from the city, Diane and I found a 23-acre farm with a very old farmhouse. We thought it would make the perfect retirement home for our little family of five. After weeks of negotiating by phone, we finally signed a purchase agreement. It was time to tell the dogs. That night, we turned off the TV early.

Mozart turned to look at me. "Hey what's up, Dad?"

"We want to tell you guys something."

"Oh boy! A family meeting," said Whoopi, as she jumped onto my lap.

"We won't be staying at The Residence Inn the next time we go to Baltimore."

"Why? Did they find out what I did in the bathroom?"

"No, Elvis. I cleaned that up before we left. The next time we go to Baltimore we are going to stay in our own house."

"We're going to take our house with us? That will be so cool. The last time we went to Baltimore we passed a guy who was pulling his own house."

"Well, Whoopi, this is a little different. That was a mobile home he was pulling. We bought a house in Baltimore and we will live in it whenever we go there."

"We have a new house in Baltimore and we are keeping this house?"

"Not exactly, Mozart. First, the house in Baltimore is not new, just new to us. It was built about 150 years ago. It is on a farm and there are several other buildings on the farm as well. One of those buildings was built in 1821, which makes it one of the oldest buildings in America."

"Who lives in the other buildings?"

"Nobody does, Whoopi. Farms often have several buildings—barns, silos, stables...We'll show them all to you the next time we go to Baltimore."

"Can we go tonight? I can be packed in ten minutes."

"I'm afraid not, Mozart. We'll get there soon enough."

"There's one other thing we wanted to tell you guys. Now that I'm in my late 50s, I am going to retire within the next couple of years."

"Good idea. Let's retire early tonight. I want to dream about our new house and the farm."

"I don't mean that kind of retirement, Whoopi. I mean I will stop going to work every day. It will mean some very big changes for all of us."

Now Mozart jumped into my lap. "So every day will be like Saturday and Sunday. We can go to the park every day and you can play games with us all day."

"There will be a lot more days like Saturday and Sunday, Mozart. But there will be a lot of things for us to do to get ourselves adjusted to being retired. We'll want to find some place in Baltimore where we can do volunteer work, and Mom and I will do some traveling, but it will be a lot less than I do now."

"Wait a minute," said Mozart, "what was that middle thing? You said 'do volunteer work' in Baltimore. Don't you mean Indianapolis?"

"No, Mozart, I mean Baltimore. We are going to sell this house and move to Baltimore to live on the farm full-time."

After that, their comments and questions rattled out rapid-fire: "But, all our toys are here. So are our bed and the TV and everything. Is Tojo coming?"

"What will happen to the ducks?"

"How will we get to play in the park?"

"Is there a park near the farm?"

"Are we going to become farmers?"

"I don't know the first thing about farming..."

Finally, I said, "Okay, okay, lighten up. First, when we go to Baltimore next month for Christmas, we are going to buy a bed and a little furniture and stay in the farmhouse. It will be a long time before

82

I retire, and when I do, we will take everything in this house with us. There are a lot more rooms in that house than we have in this house."

"Will we have to learn to be farmers?"

"No, Mozart. It is not an active farm, and we are not going to become farmers. The entire farm is like a park, only infinitely bigger, with a woods, and hills, and a pond. Tojo and the ducks aren't coming, but there will be plenty of new animals for you to bark at."

"It sounds too good to be true."

"Whoopi, have I ever steered you wrong? You are going to love it."

"One last question...We won't become barnyard animals, will we?" asked Mozart. "After all, we are registered Canine-Americans."

"You'll always be Canine-Americans, Mozart. Although I've often thought there was some barnyard animal in each of you."

Once again, they huddled near the foot of the bed and fell asleep whispering about the exciting future that lay ahead. They had no idea just how exciting it all would be.

That Christmas, we took the RV to Baltimore. Even in the cold, the dogs loved riding on the dashboard and seeing all the sights, especially those in Ohio. By the time we pulled into the driveway of the farm, around midnight, we were all pretty exhausted. I thought we'd all head straight to bed. I could not have been more wrong.

All three dogs ran out of the RV and started sniffing around the trees.

"Hey, Dad! This yard is great. There are smells here that I never would have imagined. This is even better than Ohio."

"I'm not surprised, Mozart. I think we'll find a lot of animals on this farm that you've never seen before."

"Great! Where are they? Let's wake them up to play."

"I think they are all in the trees, or underground, or wherever they go to sleep. I don't think anyone is interested in playing this late. Come on, let's go inside."

Whoopi led the others racing up the steps to the porch. It was a big, old-fashioned, roofed porch that wrapped around three sides of the house. She ran around the right side, sniffed for a few seconds, then raced all the way around to the left side.

"This porch is bigger than our whole courtyard in Indiana. Can we just stay here and play?"

"Not tonight, Whoopi. Besides, when you see the whole farm in daylight, tomorrow, I don't think you'll want to play on the porch."

Like a lot of houses built during the nineteenth century, the farmhouse had been built at intervals. And unlike most houses built during the twentieth-century, the rooms were not laid out in a neat pattern. From the front door of our house in Indiana we could see through to the large picture window at the back of the house and through it to the lake beyond. From the front door of our Maryland farmhouse we walk in a circuitous pattern to get almost anywhere. For instance, to get to the kitchen from the front door, we walk through the hall to the family room, turn left into the formal dining room, turn right into the butler's pantry, walk through to the informal dining room, and finally, walk into the kitchen. I mention this because, to me, this is a little less convenient than a straight shot down the hallway to a kitchen or some other room. To a dog, this is heaven.

I opened the front door and we entered. The dogs immediately ran in different directions, barking. I carried the luggage upstairs where Diane was already making up the bed. I came back down, using a second set of stairs that end in the butler's pantry towards the back of the house. I ran into Elvis who was coming around the corner.

"How did you get here, Dad? I didn't see you come by me."

"I came down the back stairs, Elvis."

"What do you mean, back stairs? The stairs are by the front door."

"Look behind this door. There are stairs back here as well."

"Whoever heard of two sets of stairs? Why would anyone want that?"

"This part of the house was built many years after the front part and the stairs were added then. I'm sure they come in handy from time to time."

"This is like a secret passage, isn't it?"

"It's only secret from Mozart and Whoopi. The rest of us know about it. By the way, where are they?"

"Mozart is sniffing as always. It's what he does best. He's up front in the living room and Whoopi just ran up the stairs to see how Mom is doing. Let's not tell them about the secret stairs."

"Okay...I have a better idea. We'll hide on the stairs and surprise them when we hear them come this way."

I picked up Elvis and opened the door to the stairway. We sat down on the second step and I closed the door. Since we didn't have any carpets yet, we could easily hear Mozart's footsteps on the wood floors. Elvis was shaking with excitement.

"*Oh boy* is this *great*. I never get to surprise Mozart."

"Be quiet. He'll hear us."

We heard Mozart get closer and opened the door. Elvis yelled, *"Surprise!"* and started barking. Mozart was startled and started barking. Whoopi came running, barking as she ran.

Diane had finished making the bed and asked what all the noise was about.

"Dad and I hid in the secret stairway and scared Mozart. It was really cool."

"I wasn't scared. I thought they might be burglars, Mom, and I was protecting you."

Whoopi laughed. "You sure sounded scared, Mozart. And your hair was standing straight up. You looked like Don King."

Diane picked up Mozart and said, "I'll carry you upstairs to bed as a reward for protecting me."

Whoopi raced ahead and was up the stairs before we even reached them. I picked up Elvis and walked up behind Diane and Mozart.

Mozart looked over Diane's shoulder at Elvis. "You might want to sleep with one eye open tonight, Elvis. We'll see how funny you think it is to be scared."

When we reached the top of the stairs, we put them down. This was the first time Mozart and Elvis had been upstairs. There were four bedrooms and two bathrooms on the second floor. Whoopi took them on a tour. The dogs came back to our bedroom a few minutes later. Mozart had already forgotten about being surprised by Elvis and they were chattering away about what they had seen. We had brought the little dog steps with us and they ran up the steps onto the bed.

Whoopi asked, "What is behind the two closed doors in the hallway, Dad?"

"Stairways leading to two different attics, one in the front of the house and one in the back."

She jumped up, "Let's go see them."

I grabbed her. "Not tonight. Let's go to sleep."
I turned out the lights. In the dark I heard, "Hey, Dad..."
"Yes, Mozart."
"Why don't you retire tomorrow?"
"Goodnight, Moz..."

CHAPTER SEVENTEEN

The next morning, the dogs arose pretty early. All were anxious for the grand tour. Whoopi jumped on my chest. "Up and at 'em, Dad!"

"What are you, a cat? Go back to sleep."

Mozart pushed his nose against my face. "Come on, Dad. Let's go see the farm."

"Okay...We'll go right after breakfast."

"Let's skip breakfast. We've never seen a barn before and we're ready to go."

Elvis chimed in. "Mozart, you never said anything about skipping breakfast. I think the barn will still be there after we eat."

"Elvis, you won't have to skip breakfast. I'll take you on a quick tour while Mom gets it ready," I said.

I got dressed and we went out. It was quite cold and this was going to be a very quick tour. We walked around the RV parked in the front.

"Here's the driveway we came in on last night. It's a quarter mile to the street. You can't see it, but if you cross that bridge over the creek, the street is just past that line of trees."

"Let's go down there first."

"No, Mozart. It's too cold and it would take too long." We walked around the house. "That fence, past this big field, is the southern edge of our property. That neighbor has a couple of pretty big dogs."

"Better check it out right away, Dad. I need to let them know there's a new sheriff in town."

"Mozart, it's still too cold, and those dogs are as big as Tojo. I think they'll retain the sheriff badges for a while." We walked around to the back. "Down this hill and past those hedges is a pond. But it only gets a couple of ducks once in a while."

"Come on, I'll race you to the pond. We'll tell them we are close friends of their cousins in Indiana."

"Maybe later, Mozart. It's too far and too cold."

"Hey, Dad..."

"Yes, Mozart."

"You need a warmer coat."

"Very funny, Mozart."

"I'm not kidding. That *too cold* routine isn't going to cut it down on the farm."

"I'll dress warmer after breakfast. Let me show you the north side of the house. Then we'll head in for breakfast."

On the north side of the house, there were ten more farm buildings.

"Wow, what a great neighborhood. In Indiana, all the houses looked somewhat alike."

"Well, Whoopi, these aren't all houses. I told you old farms have a lot of buildings."

"What are all these buildings?" asked Elvis.

"That one up the road really *is* a house. It was used for tenants or farm workers, but no one has lived in it for years. Those two buildings are garages...That is a barn and the two structures behind it are silos. Over there is the horse stable...That building is called a gentleman's retreat...That one is a three-room guest cottage and the one over there covered in ivy was a summer kitchen. Those woods up that hill past all these buildings are ours also."

"Who lives in all these houses?"

"No one lives in any of them, Elvis. Since they are all ours, we can play in them."

"Let's start with the barn," yelled Mozart. They all raced over to it. When they ran inside, birds started to fly around. The dogs immediately picked up the scent of the squirrels and chipmunks. The barn was filled with a lot of junk, which just made the adventure all the more exciting. Their tails never stopped wagging and their noses barely lifted off the ground. Mozart took a break, racing back and forth across the barn while he barked at the birds, but he soon got back to looking for land critters.

"Okay, let's go eat. We can come back later."

"You go ahead. We'll catch up with you later," said Whoopi.

"Elvis, come on. Let's eat."

"I'm afraid I'm with Whoopi this time. Catch you later."

Mozart never even bothered to answer. He was deep in concentration.

"Come on, Mozart."

"Can't you see my tail wagging? That means *do not disturb*. I am closing in on one of the farm critters."

"I thought you said that when your tail wags it means you are excited or happy to see me."

"You have to learn the subtle nuances. I'll teach them to you later."

Eventually, I rounded them up and brought them into the house. They ran to Diane, shouting all at once: "Hey, Mom, we have a really cool barn! And a pond and a woods! There are lots of buildings and we can play in all of them."

"We have big dogs for neighbors!"

"We smelled lots of animals in the barn, but they're all hiding."

"We'll find them later!"

"You need to get Dad a warmer coat."

"Here's your breakfast," said Diane.

They ate every bite of it. Even Whoopi ate hers.

When Diane and I returned from visiting the kids, we went back to the barn and stayed until all three dogs were exhausted. That evening when we were all in bed, they nestled close to Diane.

"So, how do you guys like the farm?" she asked.

"This was the most fun I've ever had in my whole life. I never want to leave," said Elvis.

"I can't believe how big it is and how much there is to do. I could spend the rest of my life here and never see it all," said Whoopi.

Mozart had cuddled up in his usual spot. "Seriously, Mom, you need to work on Dad to retire as soon as possible...We're ready to move to Baltimore tomorrow," he whispered. "And besides, none of us are getting any younger."

"I'm glad you all had such a great day. We'll build some wonderful memories here," said Diane.

Truer words were never spoken.

We drove back to Indiana for what would turn out to be our last year there. As we made plans to retire and move to Baltimore, the year flew by for Diane and me. Time crawled for the three, little, would-be farmers.

"When are we moving?" asked Mozart for the millionth time.

At least it was better than when he just stared at me. On those occasions, I would finally have to ask, "What is it, Mozart?"

"Oh, nothing. I was just wondering if we're going back to the farm tomorrow."

We enjoyed our last summer on the lake. But the courtyard seemed even smaller than it was, and even the baseball field at the park seemed small. Everything reminded us of the 23 acres that awaited the dogs in Baltimore.

Finally, I retired and it was time to move.

"What's with all the boxes?"

"We're moving, Mozart. I retire next week and the movers will be here the following Tuesday. I have to pack our things so they can take them to Baltimore."

"Can I help? You open a box and I will bring my dog toys over and drop them in, and maybe we can move sooner."

"Thanks, Moz, but we can't leave before Tuesday, and we'll get everything packed by then."

"Do you think I could sneak a duck or two into the boxes, and we could take them to our pond on the farm?"

"Mozart, you haven't come close to catching a duck in seven years, but if you think you can catch one in our last week here, I'll give it serious consideration."

Moving day finally arrived. All three of the dogs were extremely excited. After a few minutes of non-stop barking—a warm welcome to the movers, the dogs ran to my side with the usual round of questions.

"Are we ready to go yet?"

"Did you tell them not to take the toys, that we are taking with us in the RV?"

"How will they fit everything from this big house into that one van?"

"Should we go say goodbye to Tojo and the ducks yet, or wait until later?"

"They just took the bed! Where will we sleep tonight?"

"Are you sure they know how to get to the farm? Have they ever been there?"

"They've taken all the toys and the furniture...Are we ready to go now?"

At last, everything was out of the house, and as Diane and I cleaned it, the dogs walked from room to room. It was the only home they had ever known, and not even Mozart had seen it empty.

"Wow...the house looks enormous without any furniture."

"This is really cool."

"I think it's kind of creepy."

"It doesn't seem like home without all of our stuff in it."

We took one last walk down the steps to the pier and said goodbye to the ducks and the catfish. Then we all walked around the house one last time and checked out all the rooms to make sure we hadn't forgotten anything. When we got to the living room, I lay down on the carpet and wrestled with the three of them.

Finally, I said, "Are you guys ready to go?"

"Yeah...but I feel kind of sad about leaving this house."

"I do too, Elvis. It's always sad when you leave your home and you know you'll never live in it again."

"We had a wonderful life here, didn't we, Dad?"

"We sure did, Whoopi. This has been the best home we ever had."

"Do you think we'll have as much fun on the farm?"

"Mozart, I have the feeling it will be more fun than we can even imagine."

"Then I'm ready to go."

"Me too!" shouted the twins.

So was Diane. We all got into the RV and she started to drive. We stayed pretty quiet for the first hour or so, each of us thinking about the wonderful times on the lake.

As we crossed into Ohio, leaving Indiana for the last time, our thoughts started to turn toward Baltimore and the farm and retirement and the life ahead of us. We talked during most of the rest of the trip. We were going to our new home. A thousand adventures lie ahead and we couldn't wait. In fact, we didn't. Diane drove straight through. Our stops were short, and at 3 a.m. we pulled in at the farm, exhausted, but happy to be home.

All three dogs instantly fell asleep. Their lives as farmers and hunters would begin in the morning.

PATRICK M. SHERIDAN

PART SIX

SHERIDAN ACRES

CHAPTER EIGHTEEN

The dogs were awakened by the sounds of hammers and saws.

"Dad, wake up. There are people outside making noise."

"Relax, Mozart. It's only the builders."

Diane and I had contracted to add on a master bedroom suite. We had become accustomed to a first-floor bedroom and until now, the dogs had never lived in a two-story house. Our new bedroom would be on the first floor, connected to the rest of the house by a short hallway. It would face the hilly, wooded part of the farm. While it was being built we slept upstairs.

"Mozart, it's our first day here. Let's sleep in."

"No way. Come on. We need to check out the builders and let them know that we'll be calling the shots from now on."

"I don't think you'll be calling too many shots for a while, Mozart. I'm more worried that you might get lost and not find your way back to this house."

Whoopi chimed in. "We won't get lost. We can retrace our steps and find our way back from anywhere."

"Whoopi, you've never been more than 10 yards from our home without being on a leash. Here, you could go over a quarter of a mile without leaving the property and I wouldn't even know where to look for you. We'll test your theory another time."

Mozart said, "Be right back. I'm just going to run out the dog door and let the workers know I'm here."

"Great idea, Mozart, but we don't have a dog door yet, since it is going to be installed in the new addition."

"Come on. You always taught us to be friendly. Let's go say hello."

"Okay, Elvis. Since even you are going to start on me now, I'll get dressed."

I got dressed and headed down the stairs. Diane was dead tired from driving and she never moved a muscle. We went out the front door. There were trucks and workers everywhere. All three dogs started barking and running non-stop, moving from one group of workers to the next. Some of the workers ignored them. Some smiled at them. Others even petted them. After a few minutes, all three dogs decided to go exploring. I followed them into the nearest stand of trees. It was about 30 yards from the house, next to the library.

"This is so cool. Are we still on our farm?"

"Yes, we are, Elvis. Right up to that fence over there. I don't want to see any of you crawling under that fence either."

"No need. Whatever lives around here spends a lot of time in these woods," said Mozart, as he walked back and forth among the trees, nose near the ground, tail wagging constantly.

"What do you think they are?" asked Whoopi.

"Probably squirrels—with all these trees for them to climb."

"What's a squirrel?" asked Elvis.

"Lunch," laughed Mozart.

"It's a small animal with a bushy tail, Elvis. They live in trees. I'm sure you'll get to see one someday soon."

The dogs could have sniffed around those trees all day. After a while, I said, "Let's go see if Mom is up—and let's get some breakfast."

We headed back to the house. The dogs obviously had forgotten all about the workers because the minute they saw them they ran toward them barking, again.

Diane was up and breakfast was served. Tongues hung out and tails wagged.

"Hey, Mom, we have squirrels here and we found out where they live."

"There's a woods real close to the house and it smells better than any place I've ever been in my whole life."

"We can show you where it is after breakfast."

"There are a lot of workers here and we said hello to them."

"They don't seem to know about the squirrels yet, since none of them were over in the woods."

"Don't tell them. Let's keep the squirrels our secret."

Diane had brought in their pillows from the RV and had set them on the floor. She gave each dog a hug and said, "You guys seem to be having a lot of fun living on the farm." Five minutes later, our fun lovers were all sound asleep.

For Christmas, Diane had given me a riding golf cart. Behind the seat there was a carrier that was extremely helpful for hauling wood, for taking out the trash containers, and for doing general chores around the farm. The seat was built for two people but was perfect for one person and three dachshunds. I kept the cart in the barn. We rode around in it every day.

Each morning on the farm started out exactly like the first. The dogs personally greeted each and every worker by running around and barking. Then I would ask their new favorite question. "Who wants to go for a ride in the cart?" And off they would run for the barn.

Whoopi jumped into the cart, then onto the seat, but never really cared where she sat. She just wanted to get to wherever we were going. I picked up Mozart and Elvis and set them on the seat. Mozart sat next to me. On occasions when I would set him on the far side, he would simply climb over Elvis and Whoopi until they moved and he was next to me. Elvis didn't mind sitting on the far right. In fact, he even sat on the far right when there were just the two of us.

One morning, Elvis was sitting on the grass, sunning himself and watching the workers. This had become one of his favorite pastimes.

"Hey, Elvis, want to go for a ride in the cart?"

"I sure do," he said, as he raced for the barn.

"Where are Mozart and Whoopi?"

"They are in the woods, sniffing for squirrels."

"Well, I'm just going to get the mail. How about if just the two of us go?"

He beamed. "That would be great." He loved it when he got special attention.

I put him in the cart and he scooted over to the far side.

"You like sitting over there, don't you, Elvis?"

"Yeah. I can see better and I like riding shotgun. I pretend we are in *The Magnificent Seven*."

"That's one of my favorite movies also, Elvis."

"Am I Steve McQueen or Yul Brynner?" he asked.

"You're Steve McQueen since he rode shotgun. Yul Brynner drove."

"I guess that makes sense, since Steve McQueen was the one with hair," he said, smiling.

"Very funny, Elvis."

We picked up the mail and headed back. As we neared the bridge, a rabbit ran into the bushes. I stopped and Elvis jumped down and ran into the bushes after him. Elvis stayed in there for about five minutes before he came out breathing hard.

"Did you see him in there?"

"No...," he panted. "I could smell him, but he was too fast. He ran down the hill to the creek and I lost him."

As we made the final turn into the driveway, Mozart and Whoopi came running. I stopped and they jumped into the cart. We all rode the last few yards to the house.

"Where did you go?"

"What did you do?"

"Why didn't you take us?"

Elvis was in his glory. "We had to get the mail, and Dad needed his best dog to ride shotgun. So, naturally, I went."

"Yeah, right. Did you think the cart was going to get attacked like a mail train in the Old West?"

"Better safe than sorry," said Elvis, before hitting them with his big news. "And besides, it was a good thing I was there because somebody had to chase the rabbit into the bushes."

"*What?!*" they screamed.

"Did he really see a rabbit, Dad?"

"Is he lying?"

"I can't believe this."

"Where is the rabbit?"

"What did it look like?"

"Where did it go?"

"I'll tell you all about it after lunch," said Elvis, "but first, I have to get some water. Chasing rabbits makes me very thirsty."

"By the way, Mozart, did you see any squirrels?" I asked.

"No, but thanks for asking, Dad. Why don't you just pour salt in the wounds? Elvis goes rabbit hunting and we get needled."

I picked up Elvis. Whoopi and Mozart usually jumped to the floor of the cart, then down to the ground before I could pick them up, but they were both still sitting in the cart. "Aren't you guys coming in?"

"No. We're staying here to make sure you take us with you the next time you go rabbit hunting."

I laughed. "I won't go without you next time, I promise."

Before I could set Elvis down, he licked my face and whispered, "Thanks, Dad."

Then he ran to the door to tell Diane about his latest adventure.

During the next few months we added a lot of personal touches to the farm. The previous owners had placed a sign with the name of the farm on the road by the driveway. We replaced it with a wooden one that read Sheridan Acres. Sheridan was across the top of the sign. Acres was across the bottom. In the middle was a beautiful carved picture of a brown dachshund with it's tail up and wagging. It looked exactly like Mozart.

We all drove up in the cart to look at it. The sign received immediate approval from Mozart. "That's the best-looking sign I've ever seen. That will let everybody who visits know that the farm is named after me, Mozart Sheridan."

"The Sheridan applies to all of us, Mozart."

"I don't see a picture of you on that sign."

"Why isn't the dog on the sign black? Whoopi and I are black and only Mozart is brown."

"Elvis, I had to pick one color and I chose brown because Mozart is the oldest."

Mozart was beaming. "I can't wait until all the workers come back tomorrow and see the sign. I should get a little more respect from them once they see who the farm is named after."

"Perhaps you'd get a little more respect if you wouldn't bark every time you see them."

Dachshunds bark at everybody. Every time they see you, they bark. It doesn't matter how well you know you. They bark at our kids. They bark at people they see every day. They even bark at Diane and me. They can be sitting on top of the sofa, looking out the window, see me go out the door, next to the window, then see me walk in front of the window next to the door they saw me walk out of, and bark as if a stranger has walked by.

One day, when we were riding in the cart, heading for the Back Woods, I asked,

"Why do you guys bark so much? You seen to bark even more here than you did in Indiana."

"We bark because we're good at it…We don't have one of those whining little barks like some of the dogs you see on TV," said Mozart.

"Yeah," agreed Whoopi, "and some of those dogs on TV bark once or twice and then quit. We can bark forever."

Even Elvis relished this discussion. "We're loud too," he said. "You can't ask more from a barker than good and loud and long winded."

"But it's not your most endearing quality. Most folks find it annoying."

"That's all right," laughed Mozart. "We don't mind. Once we have their undivided attention we can show them all the endearing qualities we want."

"And exactly what would some of those be?"

"Aw shucks, Dad. Don't make us tell you. It will embarrass us. You don't want us to blush, do you?"

"I actually didn't know you could blush."

"Well, it's kind of rare for dogs to blush. Since we don't mind if you watch us pee anywhere we want, lick ourselves, or hump each other, we don't' blush often, but it is possible."

We pulled up to the opening in the woods. I stopped the cart. Whoopi and Elvis jumped down and ran into the woods. Mozart continued to sit next to me. I picked him up. "You're usually the first one in the woods. You want special treatment today, do you?"

"No. I just wanted to tell you how much I like the new sign with my picture on it." He licked my face.

"Come on. Let's go into the woods before you get me all misty eyed."

He licked me again and ran into the woods.

CHAPTER NINETEEN

We didn't go to the Back Woods every day, so it was always a special treat. In the Back Woods there are hundreds of trees packed into a couple of acres. And by now, we knew that we had fox, groundhogs, deer, and other unknown animals on the farm, most of which lived in these woods.

Except for an opening that I had cut into the woods about a quarter of a mile from the house, most of the Back Woods is blocked off by very thorny bushes that are about eight feet high and ten feet thick. Beyond this barrier, the ground has never been developed, so the leaves from a hundred years ago still lay there providing a nice cushion wherever we walk. There are, however, quite a few trees that have either fallen or been knocked down by lightning, and since there are no paths or trails, it takes me more than twice the time to walk through the woods as it does to walk the same distance along its perimeter.

Going into the woods is quite an adventure and the dogs love every minute of it. Generally, we walk from the opening to the remains of an old fence at the far edge of the property. However long we stay, their tails wag and their noses do some serious sniffing. Most of the time, the dogs never stop talking, even when it's only to themselves.

"Somebody was just here. This scent is very fresh, and it smells great."

"Check this out! I think the foxes are nearby."

"This must be where the deer slept last night. All the leaves are packed down."

"Hey, guys, come here. I think I found the groundhog trail."

"Look at this. I found the deer's toilet."

"Let's roll in it."

This always gets my attention. "Don't roll in anything! Whoopi, come back here, and stay with the rest of us...Elvis, stay out of those bushes. I don't even want to try to go in there and get you out....Mozart, come back and stay with your group." And so it goes until we are all exhausted. "Okay, let's head home and get some water..."

Once, while on a family vacation, as my family walked from one end of a town back to the other, my son Jim had said, "This is my favorite part of vacations—the long grueling death march back to the car each night."

I often thought of Jim's comment as we walked back to the golf cart. The walk back was always slower and seemed longer. Their tongues hung out. But that never stopped Mozart from sniffing every inch he walked over.

Diane always had fresh, cold water waiting. After they filled up, we sat on the couch. It was always the same. Elvis sat at one corner of the couch with Diane next to him. I sat at the other corner holding Whoopi against my chest. Mozart placed himself in the center of the couch between Diane and me, his head leaning against one of us, his backside leaning against the other. We were never able to deduce if there was some significance to his selection of who got his head. He never wanted to talk about it, and it didn't matter since he alternated, but not in any particular order.

Diane usually asked, "How was the trip to the woods?" and they mumbled happily as they fell asleep. The exhaustion on their faces couldn't erase their grins. It would have been fun to catch some of their dreams on video.

The barn had not been used in many years and there was junk everywhere. Most of it was stacked higher than my head. I wanted to turn the largest section of barn floor into a basketball court, so I spent a lot of time, over the first summer, cleaning things out of the barn.

The dogs were, literally, under my feet.

Like most of the property, the barn sat on a hill. There was a lower level that was exactly the same square footage as the main floor. Access to the lower level was in the rear and on the side. Attached to the rear was a five-horse stable. The doors to the stable, as well as the doors to the barn, were always open. There was nothing of value that could be stolen or destroyed by animals and the weather couldn't damage anything either, so I left all the doors open so that the dogs could have the run of the place.

There were a lot of animals around. Timing had to be right for the dogs to see them, but I had seen chipmunks, squirrels, foxes, snakes, groundhogs, rabbits, and even a cat in or around the barn and the stable. I had seen evidence of mice, but never actually saw one. Maybe the cat got lucky. There were groundhog holes in every one of the five stalls in the stable.

Whoopi loved the lower barn and stable, even more than the woods. Elvis loved whatever Whoopi loved. Mozart often went to the Near Woods by himself.

"What do you want to do today, Dad?"

"Well, I have to do a few things around the house, then I'll probably work on the barn for a while."

"Elvis and I will be happy to help you."

"Great! Do you want to sweep or help carry things out to the trash?"

"We'll scout out the stable and the lower barn to make sure there aren't any critters to bother you."

"That's what I was hoping you'd say, Whoopi. I hate being bothered by critters when I'm trying to work."

"By the way, every time you play down there, you get filthy and covered with cobwebs. Is there any reason for that?"

"Remember when they asked Willie Sutton why he robbed banks and he said 'because that's where the money is'? Well, it's the same principal. We have to follow our noses and some of the critters that live around here will crawl under anything."

"Be sure to come back to me when you're done. Since it's mostly dust and cobwebs, I'll towel you off before you go back to the house."

"We will. We always do. We don't want Mom to see how dirty we get, anymore than you do."

Each week, we added another personal touch to Sheridan Acres. Drivers were forced to slow down as they crossed the bridge because there were speed bumps. But we were still concerned about the safety of the dogs on the long driveway. Since trees lined both sides of the driveway from the bridge to the house, I put up signs on the first two trees so that drivers would know to slow down. Both were the size of stop signs and made of metal. One had a picture of three dachshunds followed by the word Crossing. The other had the word Stop above a picture of three dachshunds. The signs were a big hit with Whoopi and Elvis.

"Cool signs."

"Thanks, Whoopi. I hope it makes drivers slow down."

"Which one am I?"

"Elvis, that's you in the middle on both signs."

"Thanks. It's a great likeness of me."

"I agree, Elvis. Now everyone will know that they are slowing down for three great-looking dogs."

"Don't you think it's redundant?" asked Mozart. "People will see the Sheridan Acres sign out front and automatically slow down, knowing that it is my farm and that I have the complete run of the place."

"Well, Mozart, we can't be too careful. Besides, don't we want everyone to know that there are three dogs here?"

"Yeah, I guess so. But you could make the same point with a sign that says Mozart and friends."

"Well, I like it exactly the way it is."

"So do we," said the twins.

Some of the other things we added were also for the health and safety of the dogs. The most important were two ramps, one of which led to the front porch. It was not wide enough for a wheelchair, but it was similar. The dogs could walk up and down it to avoid the stairs.

Elvis used it all the time. Whoopi and Mozart used it most of the time to go up. They rarely used it going down since, immediately upon leaving the house, they believed themselves to be in hot pursuit of something. Each day they burst out the door and raced down the steps, eternally hoping that this would be the day when they caught a squirrel by surprise.

The second ramp led to the landing by the dog door in the new addition. Since the addition was on the western side of the house, we took to calling it "The West Wing" in honor of our favorite television show. The West Wing sounded more impressive than it really was. Naming it that was Mozart's idea, of course.

We moved into The West Wing with great fanfare.

"I sure am glad we won't be sleeping upstairs anymore. I hated climbing those stairs every night on the way to bed."

"Mozart, what are you talking about? Most nights, either Mom or I carried you."

"Oh, yeah, that's right. I knew one of us had to climb the stairs every night. Well, I'm just glad we have a first-floor bedroom again. It's better for naps too."

As soon as the carpeting was down, we moved our bed in. We didn't want to wait for the curtains, which were on order. For the first three weeks, the bottom half of the windows were covered with cardboard. The sun came directly in the southern windows and it was like waking up in an operating room.

"Hey, Dad, what's going on? Why is it so bright? What time is it?"

"Good morning to you too, Mozart. It's 6 a.m., and isn't it a lovely morning?"

"I need about three more hours of sleep. Can you do something about the light?"

"I'm afraid not, Mozart. We'll just have to live with this for a few weeks until we get curtains."

Whoopi and Elvis slept under the sheets anyway and hadn't even noticed. Mozart usually slept on top of the blanket, but for the next few weeks he joined them.

"Move over, guys," he said, waking them as he pushed his way under. "It's going to be a little crowded under here for a while."

CHAPTER TWENTY

Living in Maryland has brought several changes to our lives. Many are the result of living closer to most of our children and grandchildren. Mary, Patrick, and Kelly live in Baltimore and Kevin and Clyde live close enough to drive here on holidays.

Whenever one of them visits the farm, the welcoming routine starts in the same way. All three dogs surround the car and bark as each passenger gets out. After a minute or so, the dogs stop barking—then proceed to ignore the guests during most of the rest of their visit. If only the dogs would sit next to them, the kids would pet the dogs, but for the most part, the dogs remain aloof—with one exception.

Mozart and my grandson Ian have developed a bond. When we moved back to Baltimore, Ian was three years old. We had a toy space gun that shot bullets that were foam rubber discs. Mozart loved to chase after them and catch them in his teeth. He caught more that had hit the ground than were flying through the air, but he was delighted either way. I shot the gun on rainy days and on days when it was too cold to go outside. Ian shot it on every visit.

"Hey, Mozart, guess who's coming over today?"

"Let me think…an electrician, a carpenter, a plumber, or all of the above?"

"Very funny, Mozart. Mary and Jeff are coming with Ian and Abby."

"Great! Let's go wait on the porch."

"Let's wait until we hear the car, so you don't get run over."

He went to the front door to wait. When he saw the car coming up the drive, he started barking. I opened the door and Whoopi and Elvis joined Mozart in racing to the car. They barked wildly as they ran.

"Hi, Ian! Let's go shoot the gun."

"Mozart, leave Ian alone for a while. He hasn't even taken off his coat yet."

On the farm, there are many things for Ian to do and to play with—shooting the gun for Mozart was only one of them. In Mozart's mind, there was no question what the top priority should be.

"Dad, where's Ian?"

"He's in the barn playing basketball."

"Does he know the gun is in the living room?"

"I'm sure he does Mozart. It always is."

"Should I go get him?"

"No. He'll be along in a minute. Be patient."

Eventually, Ian came inside and picked up the gun, loaded the discs into it, and started shooting. Mozart could be heard throughout the house, running and barking. When I went to check on how they were doing, Mozart was out of breath, grinning from ear to ear, and waiting for the next shot.

"How are you guys doing?"

"Granddad, this gun stopped shooting."

"Are those fresh bullets?"

"No...I shot all of them once and they were fine. But now they won't come out."

"They won't come out because Mozart gets them all wet, and when they're wet, they stick in the gun. They have to dry off for a day or so before you can shoot them again."

"Do you have any more dry ones?"

"Actually, I do. I have a box of them on a shelf in the laundry room."

I gave Ian a handful and he shot all of them for Mozart. After that, Mozart was completely exhausted. He lay on the floor with three discs in his mouth, slowly chewing. His eyes were closing. Ian went upstairs to the toy room to play with Diane and Abby.

"Did you have fun, Mozart?"

"Sure did. Ian's a great shot. I caught three bullets in the air."

"Three out of about fifty...that's pretty good, Moz."

"Ian shot twice as many as you usually do. When were you going to tell me about the extra box of bullets in the laundry room?"

"Until Ian asked me for more, I actually forgot that they were there."

"Thank God for Ian," he said and promptly drifted off to a very sound sleep.

The first time Diane and I left the house to visit one of our kids, it brought a very interesting reaction from the dogs.

"Why are you getting dressed up?"

"We are going over to Mary's house."

"Are you taking us with you?"

"No, I'm not, Mozart. But we won't be gone too long. You can go outside to the backyard if you want to. We'll leave the dog door open."

"I'd rather go with you. I could take the gun and play with Ian."

"I'm sure you would rather go with us, Mozart, but this time Mom and I are going alone."

"You said *this time*…Does that mean that next time I can go with you?"

"No, Moz. It's just a figure of speech."

Whoopi came in and saw that I was getting dressed to go out. "Oh man, don't even tell me…you're going out. You won't even be halfway down the driveway before Obergruepenfuhrer Mozart will be telling Elvis and me that you left him in charge."

"Well, he is the oldest."

"Then he'll start ordering us to fetch him his toys and to stick our heads out the dog door to tell him if any squirrels are out there."

"He's just pulling your leg, Whoopi. Just ignore him."

"Talk about absolute power corrupting absolutely."

In Indiana, I had never been around dogs other than my dachshunds. Mary had a female dog named Chloe, a very friendly bichon frise who loved to jump on my lap whenever I sat on the couch. When we arrived home, all three of our dogs came running outside. As usual, they were barking and smiling. Their tails wagged as they ran. When they reached me, they came to a screeching halt and circled around, smelling my pants.

"Whoa, Dad…Where have you been? Mary doesn't smell like this. Who have you been with? What have you been doing?"

"Lighten up, Mozart. Mary has a dog and she jumped onto my lap."

"She smells pretty good…"

"She's a very nice dog, Elvis."

"Let's revisit the subject of going with you the next time you go to Mary's house. Or at least of telling Mary to bring her dog the next time they visit us."

"Let's not, Moz. You guys would overwhelm her. She's just a little dog."

"No way, Dad. We'd be chillin'. You get her here…and just watch me turn on the charm."

Whoopi didn't say a word. After circling around me several times, she walked a few feet away before turning back to me. She just stared. Then she ran to the dog door and into the house. I found her on my bed pillow, curled up in a ball.

"Hey, Whoopi. Don't I get a welcome home lick?"

"You smell like you've already had one."

"Come on, Whoopi. You know you're my only little girl."

"I thought I was. But apparently you'll let anyone jump on your lap. And don't tell me it was all her fault. I've seen enough soaps on TV to know *that* isn't true."

I picked her up and held her against my chest.

"Ugh…This shirt smells as bad as your pants. Put me down until you take those clothes off and burn them."

"Okay, Whoopi. I'll take them off, but I'll only throw them in the laundry."

That night, when we were all sitting in bed, watching TV, and the dogs were chewing dog biscuits, Whoopi came up and climbed onto my lap. I picked her up and held her close to my face.

"Am I really you're only little girl?" she whispered.

"Of course, you are. I was only trying to be friendly since I was a guest in Mary's home. Am I forgiven?"

"Yeah…Can I sleep on your pillow tonight?"

"I'd like that very much."

We turned the lights out and she snuggled into my neck. I was back in her good graces.

Patrick and Sarah have two large dogs. Both are extremely well behaved. They don't jump on me—because if they did, they would knock me over. Patrick and Sarah also have a cat. In the course of a visit, the dogs and the cat all brush against my pants several times. After our first visit to their home, the homecoming Diane and I received was very different from the one we received after our first visit to Mary's house.

"Hey, Elvis, get a load of this…I haven't smelled anything this good since I was a kid and went to camp. Dad, did you visit a pet store or what?"

"No, Mozart. Patrick and Sarah have two dogs and a cat, and they brushed against me."

"Dad, you should invite them over to play with us," said Elvis.

"Well, you're not ready for a cat, and both dogs are at least twice as big as you. Considering how much you bark at big dogs, I think we'll pass on an invitation for now."

I was sitting on the couch when Whoopi came running into the room. She always immediately jumps onto my lap, but this time she came to a dead stop at my feet. She smelled the bottom of my pants legs for a minute or so. Then she jumped onto my lap and looked me right in the eye. "Now, where have you been...the zoo or the Jerry Springer Show?"

I started to say something, but she gave me a look that said *Whatever it is that you're about to say, don't even go there.*

I didn't.

CHAPTER TWENTY-ONE

One day, when the dogs were out playing, Elvis sat down and he didn't get up again.

"Elvis, what's the matter, little buddy? Why won't you walk?"

"Because it hurts."

"What hurts?"

"Everything hurts...my back...my legs..."

This wasn't like Elvis at all. He loved to run and play. But dogs, like children, won't walk if they break a leg or if walking causes severe pain. Only "grown-up" humans will try to walk to see how much pain it will cause.

Elvis wouldn't move, and since Diane and I had both undergone surgery for ruptured disks, we recognized his symptoms. We could only hope that we were wrong. We weren't. Diane and I smothered him with love and affection and carried him everywhere. Surgery for his ruptured disk would have to be done immediately.

Elvis had never shown fear when he went to the vet's office, and he didn't show it that day either. But he really didn't want us to leave him and it broke our hearts to do so. He stayed in the hospital for several days and we visited him every day.

"Hi, Mom and Dad. It's great to see you. Are you taking me home today?"

"Hi, Elvis. How are you doing? That's a big bandage you have there. Runs the entire length of your back. Still can't wag your tail, I see."

"They have me pretty drugged. I can't wag anything. Are you taking me home today?"

"Not today, Elvis, but soon. Mozart and Whoopi said to say 'Hi.' They miss you. Whoopi just walks around with a long face all day and looks everywhere for you."

"I miss them, too. I sleep a lot here, even more than I do at home."

"It's the drugs, Elvis. They make you sleepy, but they get rid of the pain."

"Will you take me home tomorrow?"

"We sure hope so. We love you very much, and living on the farm is no fun at all—for any of us—without you there."

Elvis never complained, but every visit was the same and every visit broke our hearts. When we were finally allowed to bring him home, we put him in a crib in our bedroom. For a long time, both Whoopi and Mozart acted somewhat afraid of him. We were never able to tell if they thought that they might accidentally hurt him or if they were worried that they might catch what he had. Either way, compared to the old days, they were ill at ease around him.

It was supposed to take a few weeks for him to start walking again, but months passed and he still couldn't walk. He also had no control of his bladder and bowels. However, through all of this, he never lost his spirit. If we left him in the crib too long, while the rest of us were in the living room or outside, he let us know he didn't appreciate it.

"Elvis, this room is a mess. There's foam rubber everywhere. What did you do?"

"I was bored, so I made up a game."

"Exactly what game was that?"

"I bit off chunks of the mattress and tried to see how far I could spit them through the bars of this crib."

What's left of that mattress is now a pad in the back of the golf cart; it keeps my tools from rattling against the metal.

The veterinarians were a little surprised when Elvis had not recovered after a few months, but we were determined to take as long as needed to see him walk again. One day, after finishing his swim therapy, he stayed on his feet for the first time and took a few steps. After swim therapy the next time, he took a lot of steps. Finally— months after the veterinarians thought he would—Elvis started to walk again. When we got home that day, he waddled toward Mozart and Whoopi. He walked like Forrest Gump, the early years. Whoopi and Mozart came running, all three tails wagging again. Whoopi and Mozart were completely over their discomfort with being near him.

Whoopi said, "Elvis, welcome home. How was swimming?"

"I had a great time at the swim club. You guys will have to try it sometime."

"Come on...I found out where the chipmunks live. I'll show you where their hole is."

They ran off together. Whoopi ran ahead, but kept circling back to be with Elvis. When they got to the hole in the summer kitchen's wall, they stood shoulder-to-shoulder, heads lowered, whispering. Occasionally, they licked each other's ears. Things were finally back to normal between them.

As Elvis began to recuperate, he wanted to run and play with Mozart and Whoopi, but couldn't. His strong will far exceeded his abilities. I learned this the hard way.

Our neighbors had a German shepherd that my dogs loved to race. Whenever they saw him in his yard, they ran down to the long fence. The dogs raced back and forth on their respective sides of the fence. But it was never much of a race. The neighbor's dog would run the full length of fence and back, then sit across from my guys in a taunting manner. He was much faster. My guys barked incessantly until, finally, the competition would turn its back and slowly walk away. Sometimes, he gave them a second lesson in humility by running up and down along the fence again. We always referred to him as The Big Dog.

The Big Dog was outside when I was driving Elvis around the farm in the cart one day. Mozart and Whoopi started barking and ran toward the fence.

"Elvis, do you want to go over and see The Big Dog? You haven't seen him since your surgery."

"That would be great. I'd love it."

We drove up to the fence but The Big Dog had already run up and down the fence line and back again. Mozart and Whoopi stood there barking.

"Do you want me to put you on the ground so that you can bark with the guys?"

"Yeah, thanks. I've missed this."

They were all barking when The Big Dog decided to take another run. He headed down the fence with my three in hot pursuit. Elvis was running with his front legs, dragging his rear end—back feet trailing behind. He was going faster than I could run, so I jumped into the golf cart and raced ahead to cut him off. I picked him up. His hind legs were bleeding from being dragged. I felt so guilty. He had caught me completely by surprise. I never let that happen again.

It has been a few years since Elvis had his surgery. He never would have recovered if it weren't for Diane's love and care. Elvis knows this and often says so. When Diane and I met, Diane was a registered nurse. Her experience gave her the knowledge to nurse Elvis back to health. A very close and special relationship has developed between them as a result.

The vets say Elvis will never get any better than he is now, and we believe that this is correct. Elvis still doesn't have control over his bladder or bowels, but he always sits on a pad, and by paying attention to the time, we are able to keep indoor accidents to a minimum. Elvis is much slower than he was before his injury and waddles more than he runs. From time to time, his right rear leg gives out, but he always bounces back up. He doesn't let this interfere with his outdoor play. He still plays with Whoopi and Mozart every day, and when he sees a groundhog, he moves surprisingly fast.

He has given up on chasing squirrels and rabbits.

Of all three dogs, Elvis still has the disposition that is mostly always pleasant. Even Mozart says, "Elvis is the best dog, we ever had." It's hard to argue with that.

When Diane found an advertisement for indoor ramps in a dog magazine, we bought two: one to go next to the dog couch in the formal living room and one to go next to our bed. Whoopi uses the ramp in the bedroom all the time. Mozart and Elvis use the ramp to get down from the bed, but Diane and I usually pick them up to put them on it. Diane and I both feel that, while it is too late to prevent Elvis' disk problem, perhaps it is not too late to help Mozart and Whoopi.

PART SEVEN

AT ONE WITH NATURE

PATRICK M. SHERIDAN

CHAPTER TWENTY-TWO

There are two things that frighten Whoopi, and she reacts to each quite differently. One is a thunderstorm. Thunder sends her running to me. In Maryland, we seem to have more severe—and more frequent—thunderstorms than we did in Indiana. Perhaps, because we live out in the country, these seem louder and more frightening to her.

Often, the storms come at night when Diane and the dogs are in bed. I am usually sitting at my computer in the study when Whoopi comes running down the ramp and up to me.

"Hi, Dad."

"Hi, Whoopi! What's up?"

"Nothing much. Would you like to come to bed?"

"Not yet. I thought I'd just type for a while. Is that okay?"

The thunder rumbles again and she jumps against my leg. I turn my chair and she jumps onto my lap.

"Okay, sweetheart, I've got you. I'm sorry. I didn't hear the thunder earlier."

I carry her into the bedroom and we get into bed. She snuggles as close as she can. Her head is completely buried against my neck, and it takes several minutes for her to stop shaking. She never falls asleep until a storm is over.

"Are you all right, now, Whoopi?"

"Yeah. Thanks, Dad." She licks my face.

"Okay. You curl up on my pillow and I'll be back soon."

The other thing that frightens Whoopi is something of a mystery. About once a month or so, during the day, when she is out playing, she will come racing back through the dog door and into the bedroom at full speed to hide under the bed. I ask what has happened. "Did some animal frighten you?…Did you have a fight with some animal?…"

She has never answered my questions and she has never come out for comfort. She just stays under the bed for a while. When she does come out, she acts as if nothing has happened. So far, no matter how many times I've tried to find out what has occurred, it remains a mystery.

CHAPTER TWENTY-THREE

Living on the farm, the dogs come into contact with many different types of animals. The most common encounters are with squirrels. There are hundreds of trees on the farm and dozens of squirrels.

The squirrels constantly run from tree to tree. When the dogs see them, they give chase, but never get close. I was the first to see the few that live in the barn, but by the time I called the dogs, the squirrels had run up into the rafters and the dogs could only smell them. In the old days, that was enough to make them happy.

That fall, I watched many of the squirrels store chestnuts and other food in the trees as they prepared for winter. It was amazing how many holes I could see in the trees when I looked closely. Generally, squirrels select holes that are at least six feet off the ground. But one squirrel chose a large hole—with an opening of three or four inches—that was barely two feet off the ground. Mozart was standing on his hind legs, chewing on the tree when I arrived.

"Mozart, what are you doing?"

"Dad, come here quick! There's a squirrel in this tree. I can smell him, and I can hear him."

"I can see him," I said, as I looked inside.

"There's no way for him to escape. He's been in there for an hour. If he had a way out, he'd be gone by now, right?"

"Yes…But he doesn't have to leave, unless he wants to get some sleep. You can't get your face in there to reach him."

"That's why I'm widening the hole. I can eat my way into the tree. Then I'll get him."

"Mozart, give it a rest. This can't be good for your back, and you'll never eat your way through the tree."

"Oh ye of little faith…"

I picked him up. "Let's go home and get some water. You're completely out of breath."

Whoopi and Elvis had been circling the tree and now finally had a turn. They scrambled to get at the hole. I had to go back and get them after I put Mozart in the house.

The standoff lasted all winter. The squirrel didn't leave his hole for another, and there was no keeping Mozart away from that tree. He went there every single day. The ground around the tree turned to mud on rainy days, but that didn't deter Mozart. By chewing religiously all the way around the hole, Mozart ate a six-inch-wide section of the tree. But he never got very deep.

"Where are you going today, Mozart?"

"You have to ask? Today is the day I make my breakthrough."

"Moz, you've eaten all the bark around the hole, but you're not making any progress on getting closer to the squirrel. Don't you find that frustrating?"

"It could be worse."

"Oh, yeah, how's that?"

"Well, I keep thinking about that squirrel in there, and I figure he's married, and every day he has to listen to his wife remind him that he was the one who wanted the hole close to the ground so that it would be easy to get to."

"I suppose that *is* worse."

"Yeah…It's a long shot, but I think after he's listened to that long enough, he may decide to commit suicide and come running out of the hole—and I want to be there when this happens."

The squirrel did not relocate that winter. He had his food stored in that hole, and it was either too late to move or he didn't know if he could find enough time away from Mozart to get it done. Mozart had a sore back, but the vet gave us something for pain. Mozart's pain went away when the squirrel moved to safer territory in the spring.

"Do you miss going up to the squirrel tree?"

"No. Now that spring is here, I can chase several squirrels every day. I just wish there was some way I could get closer to them so that I could make it a race."

"Well, Patrick and Sarah gave me a gift for my birthday and it might help you do that. I'll set it up."

Mozart would come to regard this gift as the best present anyone ever gave me. It was a beautiful, wood bird feeder with a glass container for the birdseed. It was designed to be hung from a tree so that the squirrels could not get at it and take the food away from the birds. But, from my observations, squirrels can get at any bird feeder that a bird can. For our amusement, we wanted to feed the squirrels more than we wanted to feed the birds anyway.

I set the feeder on the ground about ten feet from the dog door that leads out the rear of the house to our backyard, a section of land we've enclosed with a white picket fence. The old summer kitchen and four trees are in this "yard."

Many beautiful birds have come to the feeder over the years, including cardinals, blue jays, robins, barn swallows, and more than a dozen other birds that I can't identify. There are also five squirrels and three chipmunks that love to come there for a meal. Generally, the squirrels spill most of the seed the first day we've filled the feeder, often knocking the feeder on its side. So it's not uncommon to see two or three squirrels, one or two chipmunks, and a few birds all at the feeder at the same time.

"Dad, pick me up! Let's look out the window."

"Sure, Mozart. There are two squirrels out there."

He starts wriggling like crazy. "Put-me-down, put-me-down..."

Mozart races for the dog door but Whoopi almost always beats him to it. They burst outdoors and everyone heads for the trees. This is great exercise for the dogs and the squirrels, although the squirrels haven't volunteered for this program. They run up one of two trees in the backyard, across the roof of the summer kitchen, jump to a tree outside the fence, run down, and race into the woods.

Meanwhile, Whoopi goes after the chipmunks, spending most of her time trying to get into the holes in the walls of the summer kitchen or to get under the porch where they have run. The dogs finally come back.

"How did it go, Mozart?"

"I almost caught one. I ran through the gate just as he came down the second tree."

"Well, maybe next time."

"Dad, we need to talk."

"Okay. What's up?"

"I never beat Whoopi to the door. It's like chasing the ducks on the lake all over again. I know that I could catch a squirrel if I could ever be the first one out the door."

"Okay, let's try this...I won't pick you up anymore. If I see a squirrel when I walk by a window I'll just point to the door. Then you can casually walk to the dog door and you'll be out before Whoopi knows it."

"Great idea, Dad," laughed Whoopi, "but it won't work."

"Why not?"

"Try it, you'll see."

When my kids visit, they get a kick out of seeing my hand signals to my dogs. Of course, now, I don't even have to point. All I have to do is nod my head and Mozart immediately races to the dog door. Whoopi usually hears him and still beats him—even if she is under the sheets in the bed when I silently signal Mozart.

"Whoopi, how did you know that my signal wouldn't work and you'd still beat Mozart?"

"You told Mozart to *casually walk* to the door…The only time he walks casually is when you are trying to get him to come home. His name isn't Mozart Thunderhooves Sheridan for no reason. I can hear those thundering hooves from anywhere in this house."

Occasionally, I will see the squirrels and pick Mozart up from the bed—without Whoopi noticing—and carry him to the door, open it, and put him down outside before she can get there. Even then, she will beat him through the gate. But at least he has had his shot at the squirrels.

Elvis knows that, since his surgery, he doesn't have a chance at catching a squirrel, so he doesn't bother. Of course, Mozart and Whoopi don't have a chance either, so maybe Elvis actually is the smart one. The squirrels seem to like Elvis. When I go back inside after opening the door to set Elvis out to pee, the squirrels return to the feeder. They continue eating with Elvis watching from about ten feet away.

CHAPTER TWENTY-FOUR

Our favorite animals on the farm are the rabbits. We see seven or eight of them every evening. They act very differently than squirrels. While the squirrels are out all day long and run everywhere, the rabbits sit quite still about five feet from the heavy bushes and mostly come out at night. While the squirrels race for the trees as soon as they see us coming, the rabbits are in no hurry. They know that when they hop into the bushes they will be completely safe.

"Let's go chase some rabbits!" is all I need to say and Whoopi will jump to the front seat of the cart. I pick up Elvis, put him on the seat, and take off after Mozart. Mozart always runs down the driveway, chasing squirrels up the trees as he goes. When we catch up to him, he stops and lets me pick him up and put him in the cart.

Usually, there are one or two rabbits near the bridge. The rabbit will sit still, watching us as we come to a stop. Whoopi and Mozart will jump out of the cart and race toward the rabbit before I can set Elvis down. When Whoopi gets within five feet, the rabbit takes two quick hops and is into the bushes.

"We almost had him that time, Whoopi," says Mozart.

"We *almost* have him *every time*, Mozart."

"Should we go in after him?"

"Why bother? It smells just as good out here and we won't have to fight our way through the bushes. Besides, we'll never find his hiding place."

"Let's send Elvis in there."

"You've been watching too many 'Let Mikey try it.' commercials."

"Seriously, Whoopi, he doesn't mind. He loves to crawl around in the bushes. Hey, Elvis, come here."

"What's up, Mozart?"

"Be quiet, listen...I think I can hear that rabbit. He went in right here. Did you see him?"

"Yeah, I saw him go in. He always goes in right about here."

"I think he is still just inside these bushes. You go in and Whoopi and I will wait out here in case he runs out when he sees you."

Elvis headed into the bushes.

"Mozart, how long do you think Elvis will stay in there?"

"You mean, how long before Dad starts calling for him to come out...Ever since that time he went in here, crossed the creek, and came out soaking wet, about fifty yards away and thirty minutes later, Dad gets real anxious."

"Elvis, come out now," I yelled. "Come on. Let's go home! Elvis, get in the cart."

"What did I tell you?"

We repeat this ritual every night at one or two additional locations around the farm. Once a week or so, we see a rabbit in an open field and often, it will run around a good bit before it heads for the bushes. Whoopi and Mozart give a good chase, but never get very close.

One morning, when Elvis was alone, he saw a rabbit in the front yard. I watched him waddle after it. The rabbit waited until he was a few feet away, then hopped about ten feet and stopped. Elvis kept coming and again, when Elvis got close, the rabbit hopped about ten feet and waited. They kept this up for about fifty yards before Elvis just stopped. Elvis and the rabbit sat there, no more than five feet apart, staring at each other. This lasted for a few minutes. When I saw that Elvis was exhausted, I went to get him. As I got close, the rabbit ran into the nearest bushes.

"You look beat, Elvis. I'll carry you home."

"That's the farthest I've run in a long time."

"For a while, I thought you were going to catch him."

"I thought so too, at first, but I think he was just playing with me."

"Well, he gave you a good workout. Let's get some food and water, then we can watch TV."

"If it's all the same to you, I think I'll go to bed instead."

I had never seen any of the dogs come close to catching a rabbit, but one day, Whoopi caught one. I stepped into the hall, and right under the dog door, on the carpet, I saw a rabbit head with hunks of fur lying around it. Whoopi was sitting a few feet away. Less than a minute later, she threw up the rest of the rabbit.

"Whoopi, this is gross. I have to clean up this mess before Mom sees it."

"Aren't you proud of me? Aren't you going to ask me how I caught the rabbit?"

"No, I don't even care. Why didn't you stay outside? Ugh!"

"I didn't know that I was going to throw up. I never throw up. Only Mozart does that."

"Well, maybe everybody throws up if they eat an entire rabbit. Next time do it outside."

I cleaned up the mess, but not before stretching bright yellow tape around the scene of the crime and taking a couple of pictures. It was pretty well cleaned up before Diane got home. And fortunately, the carpet cleaners were scheduled to come the following week, so all traces of the crime were soon gone.

I was sitting on the sofa later when Whoopi jumped onto my lap and snuggled close.

"You didn't seem very happy that I caught the rabbit."

"Well, I was a bit shocked to find it in the house. And I never pictured you as the killer type. Here you are, my cute little pumpkin, and you're the first to kill, before either Mozart or Elvis."

"I'm a lot faster than they are. I always come closer to catching animals than they do."

"I know. As I said, I'm just a little shocked."

"You still love me though, right?"

"Of course, I love you. You're still my little sweetheart. I just didn't realize that my little sweetheart was a killer. Besides, I thought we loved the rabbits. We play with them every night."

"Hey, Dad, you seem to forget one thing…"

"Oh, yeah, what's that?"

"I'm a dog. Dachshunds are hound dogs."

CHAPTER TWENTY-FIVE

There are quite a few groundhogs on the farm. Groundhogs are fun to chase because they are so much larger than the rabbits and the dogs can see them better. Groundhogs, like the rabbits, stay very close to their holes, which are in the heavy bushes. But like the squirrels, groundhogs run away as soon as they see or hear us coming.

Most days, the dogs never see a groundhog. But the dogs will sniff around where a groundhog has been sitting. Elvis will also follow their smell into the bushes, looking for their holes. The groundhogs also have holes under the old tenant house by the Back Woods. On a few occasions, the dogs have chased them there.

One day, when Diane and I went out, we left the dogs in the backyard with the gate open. We knew that we would be home long before dark and we hadn't seen any foxes in a couple of months, so we thought it was safe. When we got home, Mozart and Whoopi ran to the door, but Elvis could not be found. We called for him and looked all over the house, in every room, under the beds and behind all of the furniture. Mozart might stay outside after Whoopi and Elvis came in, but I could not remember a single time that Mozart and Whoopi had come in and that Elvis had remained outdoors—especially not since his surgery.

"Hey, guys, where is Elvis?"

"We don't know. He never came in."

"We've been gone for three hours. Do you mean he has been outside all this time?"

"Yeah. We came in shortly after you left, and we never saw him again."

"What were you doing when you were out there?"

"We were just looking for groundhogs, following their scent, but we never saw any."

"You guys come with me. We'll take a ride in the cart and if you see or smell or hear him, you go to him and I'll follow you."

I told Diane I was going out to look for him while she put away the groceries. I drove all around. I drove all the way up to the bridge and even across the bridge to the road. I drove the entire perimeter of the farm, stopping the cart every few yards and calling his name into the heavy bushes. Finally, I drove to the pond and around the barn and the old tenant house before I parked by the Back Woods. The dogs went with me as I walked and called his name.

"Whoopi, do you see him or smell him?"

"No. I don't think he's been here."

"Mozart, you can stop sniffing around that tree. There's nothing up there but squirrels."

"Elvis might have gone up after them."

"Elvis hasn't climbed his first tree, so come on over here. Help us find him on the ground."

I had been out for about thirty minutes when I headed back to the house. He had not come back. Diane offered to join me, but I said that I would try one more time alone. Mozart wasn't any help, and since it was late afternoon, I didn't want to lose Whoopi. I left the two in the house with Diane.

This time, I walked most of the farm, calling him constantly, and thoroughly searching every place I had ever seen him: the barn, the stable, the woods, the creek. I used a flashlight to look under the old house. Finally, I headed back to get Diane.

We drove around the perimeter of the farm, ending up at the old house. Again, I looked under the house and its porch, using the flashlight. We left the cart there and walked to the Back Woods. The bushes were ten to fifteen yards thick—too heavy to see into. Diane suggested that I go into the woods and walk along the backside of the brush, while she walked along the outside. We did this and took turns calling for him.

Finally, Diane yelled, "Stop! I think I hear him." She followed the sound of his cry and said, "I think he is here. I think I can hear him crying." I was standing ten or twelve yards in front of her, separated by the bushes, and I couldn't hear a thing. I went back to the opening into the woods and walked around to where she was standing. Now I could hear something also.

"Elvis, are you in there?"

"Y-y-ee-sss..." he sobbed.

"Can you come out?"

"No. I'm st-uck-kkk," he cried.

127

"I'll get you out. Mom will stay here with you and I'll be right back with the shears."

"Please hu-r-ryyy…"

I ran back to the cart, where I keep the pruning shears, and drove back to Diane. I started cutting. Five minutes past. I had penetrated only a foot in depth. The bushes were about eight feet high, had very big thorns on very thick stems, and crisscrossed each other ad infinitum. After I'd cut about three feet into the bushes, I realized that I could not fit into the opening. I had to start cutting a wider hole.

"Elvis, can you still hear me?"

"Yes."

"I'm still coming, but this would go faster if you could come closer to me."

"I can't move at all. I'm s-sss-sorrry…"

"Don't worry about it, Elvis. I'll have you out of there in a few more minutes."

Diane continued talking to Elvis, as I was getting short of breath. About eight feet into the bushes, I could see his eyes through the thorny limbs that remained. I had to slow down the cutting to make sure that I didn't cut him, but at least he could see us now and know that his rescue was almost complete.

As I looked through the darkness to where he was, it was hard for me to believe what I saw. Elvis was stuck in a groundhog hole. Only his face and front feet were out. His back legs and his lower body were entirely in the hole. I doubt if he ever would have been able to pull himself out, even before his surgery. There simply was no place for him to go. Heavy limbs with thick thorns pressed down within an inch or two of his head. If the groundhog had decided to attack from the rear, Elvis would have been completely defenseless. To this day, I can't figure out how he ever got that far into the thicket in the first place.

Finally, having cut enough branches to pull him out, I handed him to Diane. She held him tight as I drove back to the house.

"This is the happiest moment of my life. Thank you for rescuing me," he said.

"You're welcome. It's the happiest moment of our lives too, Elvis."

After about fifty hugs and kisses from each of us—including Whoopi and even Mozart—Elvis fell sound asleep. He didn't even wake up to pee that night.

After Elvis was trapped in the groundhog hole, one of the groundhogs started straying further away from his holes and taking more chances. Two holes were under the old tenant house porch. Finally, it occurred to me that this was only one burrow with two openings—one opening was so the groundhog could escape. There were two more openings under the tenant house, as well. And two openings by a small woodshed located about fifteen yards behind the tenant house. The groundhog started to play about ten yards from the tenant house and when he saw us coming, either ran under the porch or under the house or toward the tool shed, whichever was closest. While the dogs had rarely seen a groundhog before, they now saw this one every day. He was driving them nuts.

"Dad, let's go try to catch the groundhog."

"Okay, Mozart. Come on guys, get in the cart."

"How does he always get away from us? He isn't that fast."

"First of all, once he gets to his hole, he has a tremendous home court advantage. Elvis learned that the hard way. Second, he's been here for so long that he has turned the entire tenant house area into his home court. He has numerous options to run to."

"It was a little frustrating before, when we never saw him," said Whoopi. "Now, he lets us see him before he runs into a hole. It's like he is thumbing his nose at us."

"Well, if he had a thumb, I'd agree with you."

"You know what I mean. I don't mind losing a race to the rabbits. They are faster than we are, but this fat ass is just getting on my nerves."

"This guy is bigger than me," said Elvis, "but one of these days he will make a mistake."

The groundhog always watched as we approached, then, when the dogs jumped down from the cart, he ran under the house. The dogs followed, and for about ten minutes, I could hear them barking under there. When they came out, they were filthy and exhausted, and we headed home. Nobody talked during the ride. They just panted, trying hard to catch their breath.

Then, one day, when I was in the cart and headed for the tenant house, I saw the groundhog about ten yards to the right of the house. I stopped the cart and the dogs jumped down. Whoopi saw the groundhog and ran right for it. Elvis ran under the porch. Elvis must not have seen the groundhog because, whenever he didn't see it, he ran under the porch, since that was the closest hole.

Usually, when Whoopi ran straight for the groundhog, it turned and ran back to the woodshed holes. But this time, he must have thought that the odds for beating Whoopi to the holes under the porch were good. The groundhog was correct. He could beat Whoopi to the holes, but it was a big mistake. He ran right into Elvis. I had seen this trap in *Jurassic Park*, and it worked to perfection. I could see the entire area under the porch without getting out of the cart. Elvis and the groundhog lunged at each other, grabbing each other with their teeth. Whoopi caught up two seconds later and joined in. Elvis had lost a lot of mobility since his surgery, but not his neck and jaw strength. The groundhog was larger than Elvis and twice as large as Whoopi, but no match for either—and certainly not for both. It was over in about thirty seconds. They dragged it out from under the porch and I got off the cart, picked up Elvis, and put him in the cart. Then I picked up Whoopi. I headed back to the house.

"Hey, what's up? We weren't through killing him."

"When he's dead, you're through killing him. He was dead."

"Yeah, but we were going to eat him."

"Ugh. *Gross*. You guys are animals."

"Duh, Hello!"

"Well, I caught that act when you ate the rabbit, and I don't want to see it again."

"You know we are going back there the next time we go out to play."

"It won't matter. I'm going back to bury him in the woods, and you'll never find him."

"Did I do okay?"

"You did fine, Elvis. But don't let it go to your head. Stay away from the foxes."

"Did I do fine too?"

"Yes, Whoopi, my little inter-species serial killer, you did great."

"Where did Mozart go?"

"When you jumped off the cart, he ran in the opposite direction. He figured he could get more action by himself."

"Bad decision," laughed Elvis. "Not as bad as the groundhog's, but bad nonetheless."

CHAPTER TWENTY-SIX

One day, when I was sitting in the kitchen with Elvis, I looked out the window and saw a very large turtle walking from the pond toward the creek. It looked like the entire trip was going to take several hours.

"Elvis, do you want to see a turtle?"

"I saw one once. You let it crawl around on you while we watched. It was bite- size, too."

"This one is a little bigger. Come on. We'll just take a quick look, and you can tell the others what they missed."

We went outside and approached the turtle. It was about ten inches wide. As we got near, the head and legs all disappeared inside its shell, but not before Elvis had seen them.

"What happened? Where did he go?"

"He went into his shell. It's a protective device."

"Do you think he wants to play?"

"Unlikely. I think he just wants us to leave, so he can continue on his trip."

"Can I see him in there?"

"Elvis, don't get to close."

"*Ouch!* What was that? What happened? That really *hurts...*"

The turtle had snapped his head out, bit Elvis on the nose and tucked his head back in again so fast that I barely saw what happened—and I had been looking right at them. I picked Elvis up. He had a bright red welt across his nose.

"I'm sorry, Elvis. This is my fault. I should have kept you back. Let's go in and I'll put a wet cloth on your nose."

"Will that make it stop hurting? Man, that really smarts. Is it bleeding?"

"Surprisingly, it's not. It looks like a big gash across your nose, but the turtle didn't penetrate your skin. It should stop hurting in a little while"

"How do I look?"

"Like the lovable warrior that you are."

"I can't wait to tell Mozart and Whoopi."

I held Elvis for a long time and tended to his pain. Eventually, Mozart and Whoopi came in.

"Whoa, Elvis, what happened to you?...What does the other guy look like?" asked Mozart.

"I got bit on the nose by a giant turtle."

"Elvis, I've seen a turtle. They don't even have teeth. Dad lets them crawl around on him. Seriously, Elvis, who did this to you?"

"Mozart, Elvis is telling you the truth. This was a huge, wild, snapping turtle. Not like the little turtle you saw."

"Well, where is he? No giant turtle is going to bite my little brother on the nose and get away with it."

"Let it go, Mozart. One victim per day is enough."

Whoopi had been licking Elvis' face ever since she had come in. She was making him feel a lot better than I had been able to.

"How do I look?" he asked.

"You look fine," said Whoopi.

"Yeah, you look great," laughed Mozart. "It's a good thing you can't see yourself."

The scar stayed on his nose for over a year. Two years later, when I was driving the cart and Whoopi and Elvis were riding with me, I saw the turtle slowly heading toward the Back Woods. I changed directions before they could see it. The scar had faded, and I hoped the memory also. I didn't want to risk refreshing either.

One night when Diane and I came home from the symphony and let the dogs out to play in the fenced yard for a while, I saw a large toad. The outside lights were on, so the yard was well lit. The toad was about the size of a baseball and was just a few feet from the dog door. Elvis was standing over him. The toad jumped and Elvis caught it in his mouth. The toad squirted poison. Elvis spit the toad out and started frothing at the mouth, and violently shaking his head. All of this happened in a split second. Diane ran into the house and came out with the water dish. She kept rinsing out his mouth until it stopped foaming.

"That was the worst thing I ever tasted. Ugh. It was awful."

"I know, Elvis. It was a poison. It's a toad's defense mechanism."

"Where do all these critters get their defense mechanisms? They bite you on the nose and disappear...They jump in your mouth and squirt poison...How do they learn all this?"

"It comes naturally to them, like barking and biting are natural to you."

"Well, I never heard of these defenses. Isn't there a manual or something you could read, then you could give me some warning."

"I'm sure there is, but I never expected to see snapping turtles and poisonous toads on the farm."

The toad worked its way over to the fence. I didn't think either Mozart or Whoopi had seen it, and I wanted to keep it that way. They had seen Elvis frothing at the mouth and Diane washing the poison out of him. Mozart came over when Diane had finished.

"Elvis, what happened?

"I got poisoned by a toad."

"A toad? That's a little thing, like a frog, right? Even people eat frogs. For us, one bite and boda-boom, boda-bing, they're history."

"Well, this was a huge toad and not only can't it be eaten in one bite, it can't be eaten at all, unless you want to be poisoned to death. You can ask Dad."

"I don't need to ask Dad. I saw you frothing at the mouth. But that toad story may not be the only possible explanation."

"Such as?"

"Well, as they say in the old cowboy movies, I think you got some bad liquor in you."

"Very funny, Mozart. I hope it happens to you next time."

"Why is it that only you and Dad ever see these dangerous creatures, like giant snapping turtles and huge poison toads?"

"Let it go, Mozart," I said, as I picked up Elvis and carried him into the house.

"Hey, Dad, next time you see some strange creature, can you show Mozart? I think I've seen enough of them."

"It would be my pleasure, Elvis. But I only showed you the turtle. You found the toad on your own."

"If I hadn't, you would have shown him to me, right?"

"You got me there, Elvis. I probably would have. I didn't know they shot out poison."

"Did I mention that you might want to read the manual?"

"Yes, you did Elvis. I'll get right on it."

There are fifteen or twenty deer on the farm, although we only see that many in the fall. For most of the spring and summer, we see about half that many. A few come very close to the house, but most stay up the hill by the apple trees or down the hill by a large block of salt that I've set out for them. From my window, I watch them come out of the woods and graze their way toward the salt lick. The deer only come out at dusk, so we don't have a lot of time to chase them.

"What are you looking at Dad?"

"The deer are coming out, Elvis. Do you want to see them?"

"Absolutely." I pick him up. "Here they come...Let's wait till they get close to the salt lick."

Mozart wants to see too and Diane picks him up. Whoopi jumps up to the back of the chair where she can see for herself.

The deer can see us through the large picture window. If we move too quickly, they will run away. Half of them are watching us and half are eating.

"Can we go catch them?"

"You never even come close to catching them because you bark all the way down the hill. If you could be quiet like a fox, you might get very close to them. The fox walks quietly among them and they completely ignore him."

"Okay. We've learned our lesson. We'll be as quiet as fox."

"Okay, but don't go into the woods after them. It is already too dark for me to find you in here."

"No problem...Get the camera ready. Photo op coming up. We'll be among the deer in minutes."

I let them out and Elvis and Whoopi dash toward the deer. Mozart heads in the opposite direction toward the squirrel trees. They make it halfway down the hill before they start barking non-stop and the deer run toward the Back Woods. The deer stop a few yards short of the woods to look back at Whoopi, who is circling around, sniffing the ground where they just stood, and at Elvis, who is still making his way down the hill. The deer head into the woods and seconds later both Elvis and Whoopi are rolling on their backs. I regret letting them go. When they come in, I take a wet rag and wash the smell off.

"Nice job of being quiet, Elvis. I see it really helped."

"We considered being quiet, but if you could chase away a giant twenty times your size would you be quiet about it?"

"I see your point. But, once again, you scared them off before you could get close."

"Well, what am I going to do if I ever catch one anyway? Bite him on the ankle?"

Just then, Mozart came in. He'd been chasing after the squirrels.

"Hey, Mozart, how come you never even bothered to chase the deer?" asked Elvis.

"Well, to paraphrase Dirty Harry: a dog's got to know his limitations."

CHAPTER TWENTY-SEVEN

Like myself, the dogs grew up in the city, and because of that, we are constantly amazed at the number of creatures on the farm. The fact that, during our first years, we only experienced three or four actual encounters, pleasant or otherwise, is even more amazing. Of course, I did not want the dogs to encounter most of the critters.

I had heard that all farms have snakes and that the snakes get rid of most of the mice around the barn, which is where I'd generally seen the snakes—two, large, black snakes and two, small, garden snakes. I don't believe the dogs ever saw any. When they were with me, I'd quickly steer the cart away so that they wouldn't see the snakes and go running after them. I don't think the snakes are poisonous, but since they are generally regarded as ill humored, I've just tried to keep the dogs away from them.

When we lived in Indiana on the lake, there were only a few bees and Mozart got stung. On the farm, we have countless bees, wasps, and hornets. We see a hundred bees a day, and they never go after the dogs. In fact, except for the two times that they have come after me, they have ignored everyone. They got mad at me when I accidentally disturbed their home—so I had it coming.

There are also a few fox on the farm, and of all the critters here, they worry me the most. I've seen a pack with as many as five of them, and there was one particular fox that I saw regularly. The fox come very close to the house. And generally, I've tried to keep the dogs away from them, but if I am in the cart when I see one, I will race after it and chase it back into the woods, even if the dogs are with me. I am hoping that the fox will regard our home as an unsafe place and seek greener pastures elsewhere.

Once, at night, when I had carried Elvis out to pee and turned on the outdoor light, a fox was standing about five feet from the dog door. I am not sure what kind of threat fox actually pose to my dogs. Some people have told me that fox only go after animals that will not fight back. Others have said that they will go after small dogs and Whoopi is one of the smallest dogs I've ever seen. Because the fox is so much larger and faster than any of my dogs, I worry about what could happen. If the dogs stayed together, they could take care of themselves. Alone, Mozart or Elvis might have a fighting chance. But Whoopi is just too small and vulnerable.

"Hey, Dad, can we go out to play?"

"Sure, but watch out for the fox, and if you see him, come home immediately."

"You say that all the time. Why do you worry so much?"

"I don't want anything to happen to you. I don't know what I'd do without you guys."

"Don't worry. We'll be careful."

"Yeah, right, don't worry…Okay, go play."

Early one fall, we had the longest, worst night of our lives. Thunderstorms were forecast, and when it started to get dark, it began to rain. As I brought the dogs into the house, I looked out across the big field and saw that the larger of the two foxes I'd seen on a regular basis was staring at us.

A few minutes after we came in, Whoopi jumped down off the bed and went out the dog door. I guessed that she was just going out to the yard to pee, but when she didn't come back in a few minutes, I went looking for her. I hadn't bothered to close the gate because none of the dogs ever went out in the rain. I walked all around the house calling for her, but she didn't answer. Then Diane and I searched the house, but she wasn't inside.

Outside, it was now very dark. None of the dogs ever went outside after dark. Whoopi hated the dark and was scared to death of thunderstorms, so her disappearance made no sense. I thought she might have ducked into the barn to get out of the rain and I searched it thoroughly to no avail. As I had when we couldn't find Elvis, I drove the golf cart over the entire farm, calling her name. Because of the rain and the dark, it was more difficult and took longer.

Whoopi was less likely to go into the bushes than Elvis, but I called for her there also. I couldn't imagine that she might be stuck somewhere because, unlike Elvis, she was so agile. She could get in or out of anything.

I came back to the house and searched inside again. When it began to thunder loudly, I was completely baffled. This was the first thunderstorm in seven years that Whoopi had not run to my arms for safety and comfort. I was worried sick that she might have run into the fox.

Since I could not sleep a wink, anyway, I didn't go to bed. All I could think about was the fox staring at us. At midnight, I grabbed the flashlight and searched the entire farm again. At three a.m., I searched again. In between, I prayed. Every Sunday at church, I had asked God to take care of Mozart and Elvis and Whoopi. Throughout the night, I reminded God of that and asked if he could grant that one prayer now.

At sunrise, Diane and I went out together and even tried walking both sides of the bushes, as we had done when we had searched for Elvis. Diane sobbed as she called Whoopi's name. She was afraid we would find her injured or worse. Again, we found no trace of her.

When our vet's office opened later that morning, Diane called and asked if he could think of anything that might explain her behavior— or if she had injured herself, where she might go to hide. He asked if there were fox around the farm and when Diane said yes, he told her that, most likely, a fox had gotten Whoopi.

An hour later, the sun was very high and even the woods was bright. Diane and I went out and searched the woods again. Whoopi was nowhere to be found. We were as distraught as we had ever been. I don't know if this was because we didn't know for sure what had happened to her, or if it was because we were afraid that she had met the fox. But definitely, it was because we both felt so very close to her.

Around noon, Diane went back to bed with Mozart and Elvis. I sat at my desk. When I looked down, there was Whoopi, sitting at my feet.

"Hi, Dad."

I couldn't speak. I picked her up and carried her to the bedroom. I wanted to tell Diane that Whoopi was home, but I just couldn't speak—so I set Whoopi down on top of her. She woke up and held Whoopi while I walked around to my side of the bed. When I lay down, we held Whoopi between us.

I said a lot of prayers that day and spent most of it holding Whoopi. She seemed to appreciate being comforted as much as I did, although I wasn't even sure what she had gone through.

In fact, we never knew where she went or how she managed to get through the thunderstorm or why she didn't come home until noon. She's never spoken of that night. And we are much more grateful than curious, so we never will either.

PART EIGHT

SENIOR CITIZENS

PATRICK M. SHERIDAN

CHAPTER TWENTY-EIGHT

We have all slowed down, as we are getting old. Diane, Mozart, and I are in our sixties.

"Mozart, how do you feel about being a sexagenarian?"

"Are you now making fun of the fact that you had my favorite organ removed?"

"No. A sexagenarian is someone who is sixty-some years old."

"Well, then, you and Mom will have to answer that. I'm in the prime of my life."

"I can show you the chart."

"I don't believe in those charts."

"Face it, Moz, you're a senior citizen. You use the ramps as much as I do."

"No way. I only use the ramp so you won't feel bad. And I'm not joining AARP. I wish they'd take me off their mailing list."

"Well, you've got that AARP look about you—gray hair, a few extra pounds, and you don't run as fast as you used to."

"Give me a break. I can still outrun you—even when you are driving the cart."

"Well, that's true, Mozart. Let's just say you're a young senior citizen."

The twins are getting old as well, although Whoopi still runs faster and jumps higher than Elvis or Mozart ever could, even when they really were in their prime.

Elvis and Mozart visit the vet fairly often. Elvis has a kidney problem, but his back is holding up very well. Mozart has a weak heart, but you'd never know it whenever there is a squirrel or a rabbit around. He still bursts through the door and chases them until the rabbits run into the bushes and the squirrels run up a tree.

When we are outside, everything is an adventure to all three of them, even if it is something they have done a hundred times before. A glimpse of a groundhog will give them a high for a week. When we are inside, Mozart still gets excited when I shoot a rocket or turn on a toy. His new favorite is a Giggle Rock, a battery operated ball that bounces around on rubber nodules, then stops and giggles.

"Hey, Dad, turn on the ball. Please."

"Mozart, you ate all the rubber nodules off in the first five minutes. There is nothing left to chew."

"That's okay. I just want to hear it."

I turn on the Giggle Rock and he barks and pushes it around with his head while he tries to get a grip, which he can't because only the hard plastic is left and it is too big for his mouth. He stops to grab the closest stuffed animal, jerks his head back and forth furiously, then drops it, and returns to the ball. Diane and I tolerate his barking and the noise of the ball for about two minutes, and then we turn it off. By then Mozart's exhausted and lies down. Like I said, he's getting old.

The twins have never been as interested in toys as Mozart, but they'll still pull the last ounce of stuffing out of one—even if it takes a month. We keep a lot of stuffed animals around, or I should say formerly stuffed animals, and we have learned to buy larger ones so that they will last longer.

The dogs are still traumatized when Diane and I travel. Recently, Mozart saw me bring out the big suitcase. "Oh no! You're going on a long trip aren't you?"

"Yes, I'm afraid we are, Mozart."

"When you're going on a short trip you try to pack on the sly. You don't even take out the suitcase until I've gone to sleep at night. So when I see the big suitcase, I know I'm in for a week of misery. How long will you be gone?"

"A week. Just like you said."

"I knew it. Where are you going *this time*?"

"We're going to Austria on a vacation."

He jumped up into my lap and looked me right in the eyes like Whoopi does.

"You're going to Austria? You're taking me, right? You're not telling me because it's going to be surprise, right?"

"Yes, we're going to Austria. But no, we are not taking you."

"Dad, I'm Austrian."

"I thought you said you were German."

"Check your history, Dad. Germany, Bavaria, Austria are all the same country. They just keep uniting and dividing. It goes all the way back to Charlemagne."

"Well, thanks for the history lesson, but what does this have to do with my trip?"

"It's my roots. Do you remember, when you got back from Ireland and you told me how wonderful it was to visit the country your ancestors came from?"

"Yes, I do."

"Well, dachshunds come from Austria and Germany. I should go back and visit the land of my ancestors before it's too late. As you like to tell me, I'm not getting any younger."

"So now you admit you're old. Well, Mozart, that was a splendid proposal, but I can't take you. However, if we see some of your cousins, we'll take a photo of them."

"Oh, by all means. That will be a great substitute for an actual visit."

"I'll tell you what. I'll pour a whole bag of birdseed in the feeder so that the squirrels will keep coming into the yard every day that we're gone. Will that pep you up some?"

"Okay…but I'd rather go to Austria with you."

"Well, with Elvis and Whoopi going with us, we just won't have room for you."

"What?!"

"I'm just kidding," I said, laughing.

"Don't even joke about that. You know I have a weak heart."

"I know, Moz. The vet told us about your heart murmur. But don't you worry, we're going to take good care of you for a long, long time."

He fell asleep in my arms. For the next week, we would miss each other very much.

145

CHAPTER TWENTY-NINE

Mary's dog, Chloe, died.

The following weekend, Mary and Jeff came over with their kids. They explained how Chloe had died and talked about how much they missed her. All three dogs heard the conversation, but saw how sad everyone was and didn't say anything. That night, after we'd gone to bed, they came up and sat looking at me. Their faces looked very serious.

"Dad, can we talk about what happened to Chloe?" asked Whoopi.

I turned off the television. "Sure Whoop."

"Did she really die?"

"Yes. She did."

"Why did she die?"

"Well, everybody dies—people, dogs, flowers. Nothing lives forever."

"What makes everybody die?"

"Usually, your body just wears out. When you get old, one thing or another gets worn out, you get sick, and eventually you die."

"Are you going to die, Dad?" asked Elvis.

"Yes…some day I will, Elvis. We all will. Things are starting to wear out already. Mozart has a weak heart. You have a weak kidney. I've had cancer and liver problems. We're all getting up there in years. But I don't think dying will happen for a while."

"What about Mom and Whoopi?" asked Elvis. "Why isn't there anything wrong with them?"

"Well, you know Mom always says that women are the stronger sex."

"You got that right," Diane said, and went back to reading her book.

"So we're going to die too?"

"Yes, Elvis. Some day we all will, but not for a while."

Until now, Mozart had just listened. "Well what happens after we die?"

146

"There are different points of view on that, Mozart. The prevailing one is that if you've been good, you'll go to someplace special to be with God. Around here, most folks call it Heaven."

"Will you go to Heaven?"

"I hope so. I try to be pretty good most of the time. I could be a lot better. I've always made people laugh, so maybe God will let me in to help lighten up the place."

"Will we go to Heaven?"

"Mozart, it wouldn't be much of a Heaven without you guys there. I bet God's been telling his friends that he can't wait to meet those three Sheridan dogs."

"Well, I hope he can wait."

"Point well taken, Mozart. I was using it as a figure of speech."

Whoopi asked, "How do you feel about all this? Are you sad when someone dies?"

"It depends. I think when a young person is killed or a puppy is run over by a car, I feel very sad. I think about all the things they could have done if they had lived longer, but I don't feel sad when an old person dies."

"Do you worry about dying?"

"Not at all. I have been very lucky. I've had more fun than anyone has a right to have. The last ten years with you guys has been Heaven on Earth for me. So no matter what happens to me now, I have no complaints."

"That's how I feel too," said Mozart. "I loved our life on the lake in Indianapolis, but these last several years on the farm have been beyond belief. I can't imagine anyone has ever had more fun than us."

Elvis and Whoopi nodded in agreement. Then they scratched around the bed, made themselves comfortable, and went to sleep.

The following afternoon, I was at my computer when the dogs came in from playing and sat down on the carpet in the study.

"You've been on the computer a lot lately, Dad. What are you typing?"

"Well, Whoopi, if you really must know, I've been writing a book."

"What's it about?" asked Mozart.

147

"It's about you guys. It's called *Bottle-Cap Sundaes.* I talk about some of the things we've done together and the discussions we've had regarding those events."

"Dad, some of those conversations were confidential. I don't think we want people to know about all of the things we've done or talked about."

"Don't worry, Mozart, I think I've been evenhanded about everything."

"Can I edit it?"

"No. You'll just have to trust me on this one."

"When will it be published?"

"I'm a long way from that, Whoopi."

"I suppose I'll have to go on a book-signing tour since I'm obviously the main character," said Mozart.

"Mozart, you're one of three main characters. And you don't have to hold open any dates for the book-signing tour just yet."

"Will they make it into a movie?"

"I don't think so, Elvis. First, I have to finish writing it. Then I'll try to get it published."

"Well, if they do make it into a movie," said Mozart. "I don't want to be played by Eddie from 'Frasier.' That dog has no sense of humor."

"I'd like to be played by the real Elvis."

"Elvis, I don't think they cast humans to play the roles of animals."

"What about *Planet of the Apes*?"

"Good point. I forgot about that. But Elvis is dead, and I don't think they cast dead people to be in movies."

"Don't be too hasty," said Mozart. "Charlton Heston was in *Planet of the Apes*. Talk about a dead man walking..."

"He's not that bad, Mozart."

"Not bad? They could have taken the gun from his cold dead hands twenty years ago."

"Enough about that. I will read the book to you when I'm finished."

"That will be fun," said Whoopi.

"Everything I do with you guys turns out to be fun."

One night not so long ago, when we were all sitting in bed, Diane and I were reading and the dogs were gnawing on their dog chews. Then Whoopi finished hers and came up to see me.

"What are you reading?" she asked.

"I'm looking at my will. I want to see if I need to change anything."

"What's a will?"

"It's a way for people to make sure that, after they're dead, the things they own go to the people they want them to go to."

"Now who's dying?" she asked, as Mozart and Elvis brought their dog chews up and sat by me.

"Nobody's dying. A will is usually prepared years in advance of anyone dying."

"What will happen to us if you die before we do?"

Mozart had been chewing and half-listening, until now. "I don't even have to ask what happens to my farm if you die, do I?" asked Mozart.

"To your farm?" I asked.

"Yes. The Mozart Sheridan Acres farm. We've been through all this before when the sign was put up."

"Well, I'm glad you asked, because the answer to your question and to Whoopi's question is the same."

"I'm all ears."

"And what lovely ears they are. If either Mom or I die, nothing changes. The survivor stays here on the farm with you guys."

Now Elvis stopped chewing and looked up. Apparently this was of sufficient interest that he didn't want to hear Mozart's edited version later.

"If we both happen to die together, like in a plane crash, then Kelly will come here to live and will take care of you. Is that okay with you guys?"

"Absolutely," said Whoopi. "I like Kelly. She is very nice to us."

"Me too," said Elvis. "Kelly likes dogs, and I like it when she pets me."

"Kelly's fine," said Mozart, "but I want to hear more about my farm."

"Kelly will live here with you until you all go off to college."

Mozart laughed. "Yeah, like Elvis is going to get into college."

"Hey, I don't even want to go to college," said Elvis.

"Seriously, Dad, none of us are going to college," said Whoopi.

"Then I guess you'll all be here for quite a while."

"Will Kelly leave the sign up?"

"You sure are fixated on that sign, Mozart. Actually, Kelly gave us the picture of the brown dachshund, which we used for the sign. So I think she'll leave the sign alone."

"Well, don't die any time soon, Dad."

"I don't intend to, Elvis."

"This is the second time this week that we've discussed dying. Is there anything you're not telling us, or is this just something senior citizens talk about?" asked Whoopi.

"I suppose senior citizens talk about it more than younger people. Don't worry about it," I said. "Life is like riding an elevator. One day the operator will say, 'Next stop Heaven.' And it will be our turn to get off."

We sat in silence for a minute. Finally, I said. "It's supposed to be a beautiful day tomorrow. Anybody want to ride the cart to the Back Woods to see if we can find out where the groundhogs have been hiding lately?"

They all sat up grinning. "Yeah. Absolutely."

"Then you better get some sleep and be prepared for battle when we wake up."

"Groundhogs, here we come," they said in unison.

Elvis waddled to the foot of the bed. Mozart lined up against me, then flopped against my back, and Whoopi lay down with her face against mine.

"And no more talk about dying," I said. "Let's just live life to its fullest every day."

Whoopi licked my face and said, "Thanks Dad."

Within minutes, they were all asleep, dreaming of tomorrow's adventures. It was then that I remembered the folly of preaching to the converted. These were the last three creatures on the planet who needed to be told to live life to its fullest.

ACKNOWLEDGEMENTS

I would like to thank Margaret Osburn for her
assistance in editing this book and
Diane Sheridan for her encouragement and inspiration.

ABOUT THE AUTHOR

PATRICK M. SHERIDAN was Executive Vice President and Chief Financial Officer of a Fortune 500 company prior to beginning his writing career. He is a graduate of the University of Notre Dame, served as an officer in the U. S. Army, and was a candidate for U. S. Congress. He has extensive experience as a public speaker and humorist. This is his first novel. He lives in Maryland with his wife Diane and their three dachshunds.